SMALL
STEPS
TO
GIANT
LEAPS

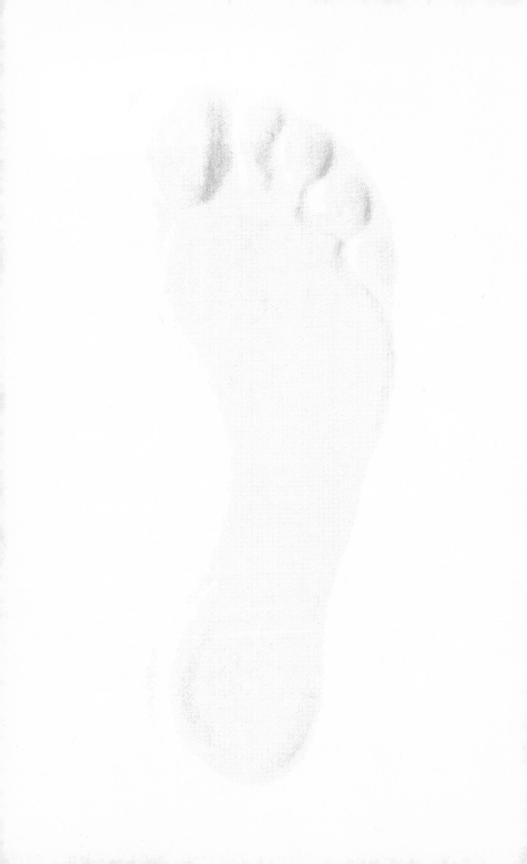

SMALL
STEPS
TO
GIANT
LEAPS

Overcoming Self-Limiting Beliefs that
Impede you on Your Path to a Fulfilling Life

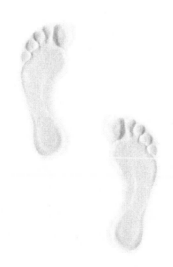

— BRIAN E. MILLER —

Author Website: www.BrianEMillerbooks.com

*Dedicated to the memory of **Doris Lehnberger**, whose infectious joy has taught us that in any moment we can stop and sing from our hearts. May your joyful whistle permeate eternity.*

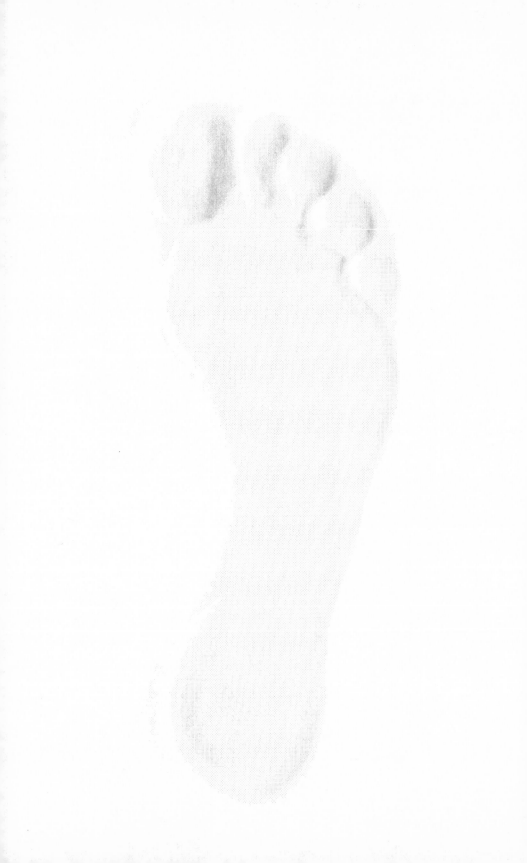

Acknowledgments:

Writing this book has reminded me of the truth of our interconnection, that there are no original ideas: we all just play off of each other for eternity in our own unique styles of expression.

Thank you to all of my teachers—both living and passed—for helping me to express and explore who I truly am, limitless. Thank you to my close friends and family, who have often been my greatest teachers, my greatest challenges, and have given me the opportunity to train in what I teach every day. You have truly been my greatest meditations.

To my students, who are also my teachers and keep me on my path.

To my father, who has believed in me even when I have doubted: truly you have been my number one fan and a great teacher.

To my mother, who has taught me great compassion and the true value of love and has always been there for me—no matter what.

To everyone and everything who has shaped me and allowed me to express my truth.

Thank you.

Brian E. Miller

CONTENTS
PART 1

PART 2

Action and Intention, Sowing the seeds for a New Garden   **111**

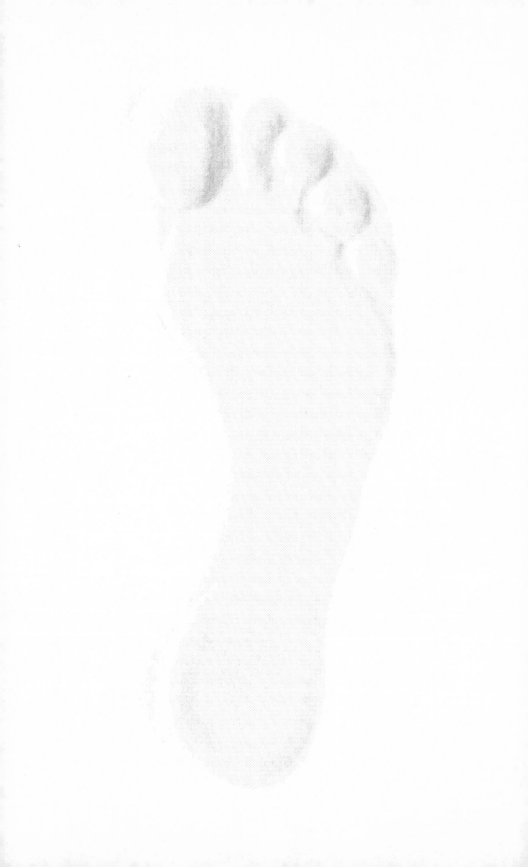

Life isn't about finding yourself. Life is about creating yourself.
George Bernard Shaw

PART 1

INTRODUCTION:

We are all looking for happiness, love, abundance, and joy in our lives—in whatever forms that may take. It doesn't take a genius to realize that we would like to experience abundance rather than lack, love rather than hate, and joy rather than sadness, but did you know that the one thing that either enables you or impedes you from experiencing this in your life is yourself? Within the pages of this book we will be delving into cutting-edge science and demystifying ancient wisdom to give you simple, practical tools that will help you to create whatever you wish to experience in your life. The truth is that your reality is the result of the habits you have created from the views and beliefs that have conditioned your mind since childhood. We often have vision boards or affirmations that don't achieve the results we set out with because these tools are useless if our beliefs counteract what we wish to experience or create. Within the pages of this book, you will learn how to get to the root of your beliefs and not only change them but also learn how to manifest the life you wish to experience.

The title of this book, *Small Steps to Giant Leaps*, implies that we work with one habit or result in our lives and move forward from there. Those small successes will create larger ones and, in effect, all large successes are the result of patient and persistent smaller successes. Big changes start with small steps.

Many times we get so caught up with everything in our lives that we try to tackle all of our hardships and issues at once, becoming overwhelmed, and then give up. We think that we can't change and that manifesting our desires is not possible. Well, not only can we change, but as we will soon learn, change is what is happening on a constant basis. We will be learning to be the conscious creators of our lives, we will learn how to direct that change in our lives as opposed to being slaves to an unconscious reactive mind that seems to just have things *happen to us*. Whether we are aware of it or not, we are creating our lives in each moment. This simple yet powerful realization will not only propel you forward to be successful in all you do, but will also allow you to relax and accept who you are in this very moment, knowing that you can create what you wish to experience. Realizing that all things change, we must accept the fact that the *self* is a process. Although this is disheartening to us because we realize that we are temporal, finally this is good news because the limited, fixed *self* we often relate to is just an idea—and one that goes against all the science of who you are.

This being said, we can use this process of change and tap into our limitless potential. Within this book we will be doing exactly that. I advise that you pick one habit or result in your life and work with it for a couple of weeks, or however long it may take. At the end of the year you may have changed ten or twelve disempowering habits in your life to empowering habits—thus manifesting the experiences you wish to show up in your life. This will be amazing, considering most people will go halfway and give up, resulting in little or no change in the direction they wished.

Take one thing and use the techniques you will be learning and see your life change as you learn to change in amazing ways. As you overcome self-limiting views of yourself, you will be empowering your mind for success in whatever form that means for you.

As you practice the techniques within this book you will find that your vibrational energy will shift from lower vibrations (such as worry, anger, and so on) that lower immune function and weaken muscle tissue, to vibrations that strengthen us and allow us not only to change ourselves but the world around us as we become positive influences.

Truly you can be, do, and have anything you wish in your life. We are here on this Earth to experience. And it is up to you what you wish to experience. There are so many stigmas when it comes to the outer-world experience, especially in so-called spiritual circles, yet there is nothing wrong with having more money, better relationships, and other things in our lives. It's how we view those things and the intentions behind wanting them.

More money in our lives may mean less anxiety and stress, the ability to help others or create projects that help others. There is nothing wrong with money, it's just a piece of paper, just an idea, but if the intention for having more money is based on greed, then not only will that greed be an impediment to creating more money in your life but the money you do create will serve to create more greed, worry, and tension in your life. You can apply this to anything you wish to create in your life, as you will soon learn. And you will see that manifesting is simple: with the right intentions you can create a life full of immense joy, abundance, love, or whatever else you wish to create, it's up to you.

You will find that I draw on the wisdom of many masters within this book, and although some of them can be linked to different religions, this book is in no way a religious text or meant to deter one or bring one to a religious study. The techniques here are simply ones that have worked for me. My life has been trial and error, and I have found that these simple techniques have helped me to grow in leaps and bounds as they have many others as well, including my students and many before us.

In this book, we will be working with the mind, an amazing creation tool. Like anything in life, if we wish to become good at a chosen task, then it is often a good idea to study those who have mastered it. If I wish to become a good basketball player, it may be wise to study Michael Jordon a bit. Likewise, I have drawn on the wisdom of many masters in this book who have mastered the mind and all its functions.

I have found that in life there are three phases of mastery. Simply put, here they are:

1. *The innocent phase is the phase of not knowing, when you come into learning something, be it a sport, an instrument, a certain practice, writing, painting, or anything. This is the primitive phase, where you are willing to learn but know little or nothing about it yet.*

2. *The learning phase is the mechanical phase, when you learn all the techniques and fundamentals, you practice hard and develop your skills based on your teachers' instructions or a book or however you receive your instruction.*

3. *The spontaneous phase is when you make it your own. You have practiced in Phase 2, and often it takes much practice before reaching this phase. Now you practice intuitively, knowing what is best for you in each moment without having to think about it.*

What we will be learning does not need to be mastered in order for it to work, in fact I have had students experience amazing breakthroughs in just one workshop. These techniques are simple and applicable to anyone. I simply point out the above to make the point that anything you learn you should make your own when the time is right.

You will see that these practices fit into your life and weave in and out of other practices you may have. I advise you not to believe anything I say just because I said it or because some master has said it. You must try it, experience it, and see if it works for you. We all have our own truth, and it is imperative that you make it your own if you are to ever get to Phase 3, which is mastery, and in essence we are all training to master ourselves. Phase 2, the mechanical phase, is always a crucial phase, so give it a try, and if it seems to be working, then keep at it or tweak it to fit your energy. It is important to have an open mind and not be cynical with anything we learn if we wish to excel. However, we must also not go to the other extreme of being gullible and doing practices that we see no results with just because someone of seeming authority has told us to do them. Remember that life is a beautiful process. Don't try to be like someone else. You can study Michael Jordon and practice his ways of playing basketball, but you must make it your own at some point. The masters can give us great insight and skills, and we should respect them for that. We will soon learn that all are our teachers in life. As we move through the process of life, we will learn to dance our style that fits into any rhythm, but is uniquely ours.

It is helpful to know that I can't really *teach* you anything. No one really can. Each one of our lives is that of self-exploration and expression, and all I can do is be a medium for those seeking their own truth, a guide on the proverbial mountain of your life. Remember that truth is experiential, so have fun, be inquisitive and open-minded, and always bring joy to your practice.

Before we begin, I want to briefly explain the word *delusion*. We will hear this word often in this book, so let me define what we mean by delusion in the context of this book. Delusion means believing things that aren't true. Examples of delusion pertain to fear, jealousy, anger, greed, and so forth. Most of what limits us and holds us back are elaborate stories, fantasies—often based on a past view that does not pertain to our current state of affairs and holds us back from creating abundance, joy, and love in our lives. Delusion is a great storyteller that often dictates our entire life. Delusions are habits of mind. We are a good guitar player because we practice the guitar. Likewise, we are good at the delusion of anger because we have practiced it. The science of neuroplasticity, also known as brain plasticity, shows us that everything we experience is changing our brain and consequently our mind. The beauty of this science is that we can direct the changes of our brain with mindfulness: what we practice will become habit and ultimately a result in our lives. Within the pages of this book we will be learning how to become the conscious creators of our lives by changing habits of mind that bring us lack, pain, and undesirable results, to habits that empower us in all we do. Clarity and wisdom provide a counterforce to these delusional habits or mental imprints. Get ready to empower your life in ways you never thought possible. To your success, be steadfast, don't give up, and always practice patience. Because with patience and persistence we will achieve anything we set out to achieve.

CHAPTER 1
DEMYSTIFYING SPIRITUALITY

Often when we hear the word *spiritual* we tend to either put on our "spiritual" hats and engage the conversation, or perhaps we roll our eyes and say, "Oh them, those spiritual people." The fact is that *spiritual* is simply a word relating to the unseen forces: the energy that governs our body and world—natural law. If someone traveled through time to our present day, from a period of time where there was no electricity, and you told them that you could put a little plug into a hole in the wall and a stream of energy would come out illuminating the room through a lamp, and oh it will also run this vacuum to clean the rug, they would look at you like you were screwy. In the least they would seem very confused, or if open minded, curious. Just because something is unseen does not mean it doesn't exist, after all electricity was always there; we just created a medium to use it and harness it, and now we utilize this force almost every second, often knowing very little about it. Likewise quantum physics and other modern sciences are rapidly proving what spiritualists of the ancient world have innately known and taught for thousands of years.

In the West, the body has been studied intensely for thousands of years, but the mind has only been briefly touched upon in that span of time. Therefore we have amazing science in ways of the body: we can relocate organs from one body to another, create false limbs that respond to the brain, and so much more. Yet we are only beginning to scratch the surface of the mind and its vast capabilities.

Many of the ancient masters utilized the mind to create a better world. One such master whose specialty was the mind was the Buddha. The Buddha was a scientist of the mind who studied the inner workings of the mind and its relation to the world. Basing his teachings on logic, he put forth a scientific spirituality that is only recently being validated and proven by our Western scientists, yet his methods have been time tested and proven by millions who have used them throughout history. It is wonderful how science is now validating what many ancient and modern masters have taught for thousands of years. Like the lamp that is powered by an electrical current, to our amazement, we can now investigate why this happens: the physics of electricity and so forth, and thus deepen our faith with logic and science and evolve accordingly. Although modern science has a long way to come before it catches up with the wisdom of the ancient masters, we can begin to easily tap into these powerful teachings and findings in our modern world and make them our own.

The Science of Meditation

Science has proven time and again that meditation can restructure the brain and rewire it for success, better concentration, more peace and composure, greater compassion, less stress, and amazing improvements in all areas of life.

Masters such as Patanjali, Jesus, Buddha, and many more have taught meditation as a way to profoundly alter our experience of life, as a means to eliminate our suffering, and as a means to cultivate more love, joy, and abundance. Nowadays, especially in the West, we are looking for scientific validation. Luckily in these exciting times, neuroscience and quantum physics are proving what those masters have taught for thousands of years, with scientific, quantifiable results. They are finding that even small amounts of meditation have profound results on the brain and actually remodel its physical structure.

Research at the University of California Los Angeles School of Medicine has given us a new look at how the brain develops. They used to believe that the brain peaks at adulthood and doesn't change from there, but with the advent of neuroplasticity we know that everything we do, every experience we have, changes the brain.

In a study published in *Neuro Image* in 2009, Eileen Luders, a researcher in the department of Neurology at UCLA's School of Medicine, compared twenty-two meditators and twenty-two nonmeditators, all in the same age range. The findings were that the meditators had more gray matter in the regions of the brain that are important for attention, emotional regularity, and mental flexibility. The gray matter makes a region of the brain stronger and more powerful. This is simply a matter of training the brain through meditation. A mathematician's brain will have increased gray matter in the area of mathematics and will have stronger problem-solving skills. The part of the brain trained creates structural changes, and thus the brain becomes better at doing what it is asked to do.

In short we can train the brain to do anything. When we are receiving negative results in our life, it is due to the habits we have trained the brain in. Using meditation, however, we can "rewire" and train the brain for success. Learning to meditate is the same as learning any mental skill: a new language, an instrument, and so on. We cannot expect to sit down at a piano for an hour and think that after that hour we will be Mozart. It takes practice and consistency, as does meditation. However, just as in learning an instrument, we can begin to see progress and change in the short term as well as the long term.

Meditation is a training of the mind. It's not some mystical practice or cosmic, New Age mumbo jumbo. It's clear-cut science and a practice that has amazing results for those who stick with it.

Researchers have proven that where you focus your attention in meditation will stimulate that part of the brain and restructure, strengthen, and make it more skillful. For example focusing your attention on your breath will restructure the brain for better concentration. It will become easier for you to concentrate in all areas of life. Meditating on compassion and love will develop a brain that spontaneously feels more connected to others. We are meditating all the time, even if we are unaware of it: the subconscious is constantly meditating on our past— over and over—and thus our actions follow, creating results in our lives. Often the meditations of our subconscious are strengthening parts of our brain and creating habits without us even being consciously aware until the results show up in our lives. Even then, we are seldom aware that the root of these results started in the unconscious mind.

We are what we repeatedly do. Excellence [success], therefore, is not an act, but a habit. ~ Aristotle

Breath meditation, or other types of concentration meditation such as focusing on an object or word has many benefits. It has been proven that concentration increases in the brain, helping it to concentrate better without distraction but also making us better at noticing what is happening around us, giving us a better perspective of the present moment, and allowing us to be present more often. The less distracting and scattered the brain, the more control we have over our limited beliefs and the easier we can direct and access the areas of the brain we wish in order to create what we want.

Sound complicated? It's not: just a simple five-minute breath meditation daily can have profound effects.

We are often so distracted and scattered that it is impossible to see clearly how we are creating exactly what shows up in our lives. In this world of ever-increasing distraction, it is even more imperative to cultivate a concentrated mind so we can begin to target the areas we wish to build as opposed to those that unconsciously strengthen while we are out to lunch, so to speak, scattered in an often ceaseless chatter of distraction.

Concentration meditation, like that of the breath, activate regions of the brain that are significant for controlling attention. This is true both for those who have been meditating for many years and for the novice who does only a few minutes a day. Those who have done this training for a while show less activation in the regions critical for controlling attention, yet research has concluded that their performance on attention tasks were found to be much better. What happens is that, in the long term, the training reduces the effort it takes for the brain to focus attention; it literarily restructures the brain, allowing focus to become effortless. Beginners can reap the benefits of this with just a short amount of meditation and progress more and more if they stick to it, eventually reducing the effort and energy it takes for the brain to retain focus and attention.

Mahatma Gandhi said, "A man is but the product of his thoughts. What he thinks, he becomes." This being said, our physical bodies are a result of our minds as well as the world around us. For example, numerous studies have found that meditation reduces stress and anxieties that cause premature aging, heart attacks, and more. I have seen a few places that use meditation as a beautification system; the results have been pretty amazing. By focusing meditations visually on the face or other part of the body—like with sports visualization combined with nutrition—people have been achieving amazing results in the world of skin care and beauty, just more proof that what you familiarize (meditate on) yourself with becomes your reality.

As we begin to see the validity of meditation in our lives, as we become more mindful, we begin to be able to see our worlds (inner and outer) more clearly and thus are able to begin to transform them. Philippe Goldin, Director of the Clinically Applied Affective Neuroscience Project in the Department of Psychology at Stanford University, shows that mindfulness meditation dramatically decreases anxiety by changing the brain's response to negative thoughts. Breath meditation is a form of mindfulness meditation, but we can also just be present and focus on the sounds and sensations around us, bringing ourselves back into the present when we find the mind drifting to the past or future.

Research shows that even our emotional responses to the world are learned habits of mind. We can retrain ourselves to be more compassionate, loving, and so on. A study on psychology done by researchers at the University of North Carolina, Chapel Hill, and the University of Michigan, found that loving kindness meditation increased the practitioners daily experiences of joy, gratitude, and hope. Practitioners of loving kindness meditation, even in just a few weeks of practice, experienced this, along with a greater sense of purpose in life and sense of self-acceptance, with fewer symptoms of depression and illness then they had at the onset of practice.

Science offers amazing insights into how meditation, even in the first week of practice, can profoundly affect our experience in life for the better. Science, though, can only go so far as to explain the deep effects meditation has on us, and in fact is far behind the wisdom of ancient masters, yet these are still exciting factors to see. Your individual experience with meditation will far outweigh any scientific study. Only you can experience your world, inner and outer, and thus the changes you will experience. We can read studies of the science of meditation or stories of the great masters' accomplishments until we are blue in the face, but all it takes is a commitment to meditate. Even a small commitment of five to ten minutes a day can lead us on a path toward profound change.

What's Your Story?

A myth is an image in terms of which we try to make sense of the world.
~ Alan Watts

All religions and spiritual traditions have used mythology to explain the inner psychology of our minds and the outer world of nature and how they interconnect. Although many religions have been perverted by corporate ideals throughout history, the base of them all is similar in that they all use mythology or story to explain nature and our role in it as part of nature. The stories we tell help us relate to and understand our worlds—both outer and inner—and not one living being on Earth is separate from this. We are all walking our hero's journey, we all have trials and tribulations in our lives, seeming allies and villains, and our stories often reflect those told in religious and spiritual traditions that are meant to teach us about and help us to understand what is going on in this life. All of our stories are interconnected in this universe or uni-verse, meaning one verse, one story. My story, for example, is a story that is the result of many causes and conditions that led up to my path and that will go on long after my body ceases to exist. My story intertwines with the paths of us all, as does each one of our lives or stories. Whether we realize it or not, what we do affects everyone and everything else. All stories are interconnected and woven together to create one story, one verse.

We are all penning our mythology with our minds. As we will soon learn, our entire reality is a result of the thoughts we think, the meditations we carry around with us all day in the conscious and unconscious mind. Wouldn't it be wise to be able to change the views and thoughts that craft our reality, the fantasies that we are creating every second on both a conscious and subconscious level? If we wish to create more abundance, more joy, and more love within the stories of our lives, then we have to begin to look at the views, the beliefs, that create these stories. Thus, we will begin there. Once we learn about the awesome power of belief in our lives, we will be able to more skillfully direct change, and in essence create whatever we wish to create in our lives. As we create more abundance, joy, love, and peace in our lives we will effortlessly project it out to the world around us because we are the world around us, all interconnected and all affecting each other.

CHAPTER 2
VIEW, MEDITATION AND ACTION

We are what we think. All that we are arises with our thoughts. With our thoughts, we make the world. ~ Buddha

Within the context of this entire book we will be using three faculties to transform our lives: our views (beliefs), our meditations (thinking), and our actions (or often inaction). These will be our main focus so that we can begin to change our habitual patterns, creating a life of abundance, love, and wellbeing. As we begin to recognize it all around us, we will learn to flow into the streams of abundance, joy, love, and so on. I encourage you to investigate and practice what we are about to learn and use it in the context of your life. Remember in all we do, it takes practice. As master yogi Swami Sivananda once said, "An ounce of practice is worth a ton of theory." We often read many books, go to lectures and workshops, and get all fired up and do what we are taught for a brief time, soon giving up or putting the practice aside. But like nature, we must be patient and persistent if we wish to be successful in all we do. Like a hundred-foot oak that started as a seedling, millimeter-by-millimeter growing to a grand oak, with patience and persistence we, as parts of nature, would be wise to practice Nature's ways.

Feel free to make all of what you are about to learn your own. Remember to make it your truth. Find how it works for you. Tweak it or leave it as it is. And remember, if you do not find truth in it, abandon it. I do ask that you give it some time, though, because it is not a quick fix or pill that will work instantly. Although you will find that there will be quick changes in your world as a result of these methods, like anything worthwhile in your life, it will take some time to work with habits you have been cultivating your entire life. That being said, using these methods, you can eradicate many negative habits in several weeks. This is pretty great considering we may practice negative habits for decades, totally ignorant of why we even do these things.

We are working here with our views that have created habits that have been locked into our minds and brains due to those views. What we are about to embark on is a system that is very simple, yet the difficulties arise in confronting the one person we often run away from most—ourselves. I ask you to have resolve and be resilient in your efforts and most important to learn to enjoy the process of change, because change is inevitable. It is the nature of reality. Like a river flowing through a valley, every second there is change. So by accepting this and riding the waves of change with joy, we create a more joyful ride. We should try to bring joy into all we do, or else what's the point? We are here for only a short time. We might as well enjoy. And as we will see later, practicing the art of joy will create more joy in our lives and the lives of those around us. When we are going through a tough time or are confronting dark places within our unconscious mind, joy seems to be the furthest thing from that moment. However, the knowledge that we will soon be on the other side of that dark tunnel and that there is indeed a light, a gift awaiting us as a result of the inner work, we can surrender and try to enjoy as best we can. The more we do this work, the more excited we become to do it. Now when I go into a negative pattern ready to purify negative, limiting, views that hold me back in life, I smile knowing I will learn and grow and finally come out victorious and stronger, enabling me to help others. Let's look at each one of these faculties here.

View (belief): We all have views or beliefs, and if we trace them back, we will usually find that they started in childhood. From an Eastern, karma-centered standpoint, they started in past lives. So we were born with the karma-based habit patterns from our previous actions before we were born. But let us work with this life, as this is where we are now. Although this is a fascinating concept and could explain why someone like Mozart could play compositions on the piano at the age of five, perhaps he was an accomplished pianist in a life before and carried the habits over, it does not really need to be thought about much. The very practical and scientific Buddha once said about past and future lives, "If you want to know who you were in a past life, look at where you are now, and if you want to know where you are going, look at where you are now." It doesn't matter what we were before this or where we are going. To accurately gauge the direction we are going, we can look at where we are right now in terms of our views and beliefs. Regardless of your beliefs in an afterlife, it does not matter. We are not concerned with matters of dogma, religion, or philosophy here, so we start with where we are now, in this current life, because for all we know this may be it. Let's not waste these precious moments, let's make the most of them.

We all have our own views and our own perceptions and beliefs, so let's look at views in a hypothetical context for a moment. What we are looking at here is our self-limiting beliefs: the views that hold us back and keep us stuck in undesirable patterns. Perhaps the view is that we are a bad baseball player. Maybe we were always picked last for the team in school. Every time we got up at the plate we would strike out. Fear engulfs us, and then we say, "I'm just not good at baseball." If you follow that view back, perhaps it started when you were young. Maybe your father threw a mitt at you and said that you stunk. Or maybe something more subtle than that happened. Maybe you lacked fathering but saw other kids excelling at the sport who had fathers teaching them. So your lack of practice that would have created successful habits in the sport, combined with your insecure view that you are not good enough to be taught like the other kids because their fathers taught them but your father is not even there for you, inhibits you. Whatever the cause of the view is, it is particular to your own situation. You created this view in your mind and then you thought about it all the time, consciously and unconsciously. And when you encounter certain situations, that's when you slip into that fixed and limited image of yourself.

The art of thinking is the greatest art of all...The thinker knows he is today where his thoughts have taken him and that he is building his future by the quality of the thoughts he thinks. ~ Wilfred Peterson

Meditation (thinking): We now have these views, which we meditate on twenty-four hours a day, seven days a week. The thoughts may go something like this: *I am not good at baseball. Maybe I'd like to be, but I am not. In fact I am not even worthy to learn.* This may seem like harsh thinking, but our unconscious minds are brutal and insecure at times, and their thinking is often very much like this, even if on the conscious level we deny that this is our core belief. We meditate or think about this mistaken view all day long, and when we encounter a situation pertinent to those thoughts, we automatically go to the fixed, limited self, without even realizing it because our minds are so habituated with it. It has been our mantra for so long, milling within the mind. And so all of our actions come out of these thoughts or meditations.

Action (or inaction): Our view and incessant thinking (even if we are unaware of these thoughts in our subconscious) lead to our actions or often inactions, our inability to do what we wish due to fearful views and so forth. You get up at bat, the fear arises, the insecurities come, and guess what? You strike out. Now this is a very simplistic example of what is going on in all aspects of our lives, whether desirable results (views that empower us) or undesirable (views that create lack and suffering in our lives). So our actions arise out of a fantasy of the past, an idea that we have about ourselves currently based on a past that does not even exist anymore. We pigeonhole ourselves; we fix ourselves in the present moment with a series of views from our past. The good news is that it's just a story, just a view from the past. It isn't who we are in this present moment because we are constantly changing. As adults, we don't even have the same bones and skin as we did as a child. Yet we still relate too much of our lives with the same views we fostered as children because the scars of our youth can linger both physically and mentally. We can, however, change the story of the scars because the story is only our version of it and only one version of many. We can view them with wisdom, realizing that we can learn from them in so many ways, and in fact they make us stronger and wiser.

This is not to say that we don't change our views sometimes. Many overcome amazing odds and prevail, but for the most part the habits we create with our wrong views, the neurological habits that create a delusion, sparking our actions, usually keep us spinning in undesirable results time and again. Life's experiences often help us to change habits, yet often it takes an extreme circumstance, and sometimes even then we don't change the habit: we just generate more fear and aversion towards something. More often than not, we are caught spinning in the same habitual process day in and day out, even when it brings us pain and results we don't want in our lives.

On the other hand, meditation helps us to direct the experiential change in our lives and speeds up the process by giving us clarity and wisdom to transform what isn't working for us. The processes we will learn will help us to change these habits, which will change our world by cultivating the view that we can change, by getting to the root view, exposing it for what it is, and practicing letting go of our limited views of ourselves. For the most part, we cycle around and around in these habits thinking *I want to change*, so we try to change and for a brief time we do but then we go back to old ways of being. And since we notice we haven't changed, each individual thinks: *I can't change*. We don't believe we can change, we have a view that we can't change. This is based on the completely false view that we are stuck with the habits that we believe define us. We mistakenly believe that we are fixed, stuck, and unchanging, and so we grasp at our story or our conditioning as defining *who we are* because even when we try to change we fail.

There is a kind of satisfaction when we fail to change, because if we are a failure, then we don't have to *do* anything. This is a laziness that fosters that view of a limited self that cannot change. Your past should serve only one purpose: to make you stronger and more successful in the present and into the future. By changing our views, we learn that we change our present and thus our future. Once we gain insight into why we are taking action in such ways that bring us undesirable results, that insight is usually powerful enough to automatically change the actions.

There is Nothing Wrong With You, or Is There?

There are many levels of mind: the gross mind, which is aware of the physical, tangible world we are most familiar with; the subtle mind, also called the subconscious, which we access during daydreams or zoning out or more skillfully through meditation; and the very subtle mind, which we access only at death, deep sleep, for a fraction of a second when we faint, and during orgasm, for a split second. The subtle, or subconscious mind is where we are open to suggestion. This is the state a hypnotist puts you into in order to change your programming, which resides in the subconscious mind. The same is true for meditation. A hypnotist is basically a guide who brings you into a deep meditation.

Our minds are in the nature of clarity, peace, and joy. The problem is that we vilify our ways of being because we do not have the ability to accept where and who we are. Ironically, this is how we stay stuck in undesirable patterns. We feel there is something wrong with us, that we are inherently flawed, but all of our neuroses, our *issues* are perfect in that moment and make us beautiful. What we are trying to do is learn not to be slaves to the emotions that arise in us, not cling to these things, and to define ourselves as such because, like all things, they will arise and pass away. We learn not to vilify or change a perceived flawed self, yet learn to accept and realize the perfection that we already are. Within that acceptance we can direct the change happening every moment naturally. This happens in contrast to staying stuck in limiting views of a self that does not change: a self that is angry or greedy or any other painful state we cling to and relate to as being who we truly are.

Psychologist Carl Rogers once said, "The curious paradox is that when I accept myself just as I am, then I can change."

Being a highly realized or enlightened being does not mean you are not presented with life's struggles. It means you see through the drama of those struggles and are free from judging them *good* or *bad*. Therefore, you transcend the pain of struggle with complete surrender to whatever is, realizing the perfection in everything. You realize that you never lost peace; it was sort of just covered up by the delusions that milled around in the mind. And so a highly realized being is tapped into that constant of peace while the world around him or her still functions and he or she functions within it with the wisdom that sees through the lies and deception of fearful, deluded minds.

There is a wonderful Zen proverb that says, "Before enlightenment, chop wood carry water. After enlightenment, chop wood, carry water." The world does not cease to be when a person becomes realized. It's just that their insight or mind is shifted to such that they see the perfection and interconnection with all and don't get caught up in the fabricated drama as they go about their lives. You see this all the time: one person focuses on and complains about all the negative aspects in life and seems to suffer greatly, whereas another person is more optimistic and seems to be calmer and not in as much pain about things as the other person. The optimistic person lives in the same world but has transcended some of the drama and in turn actually is in a better place to do something in certain situations, whereas the pessimist wastes all of his or her energy complaining and feeling impotent to do anything for anyone—and so usually doesn't.

If a highly realized or *enlightened* being walked into a classroom, or anyplace for that matter, she would see only enlightened beings, only pure beings, yet she would also see that we don't recognize this due to a veil of delusion that blinds us, creating a sense of separation and impurity, spinning in a torrent of delusion relating to a fixed, limited self.

There seems to be an epidemic of insecurity in this world. We believe we are flawed, that something is wrong with us, we relate to that fixed, limited self that is inherently broken, and as we age this view often grows deeper.

Our minds are analogous to a glass of water. If there were a glass of water sitting in front of you, you would see clear water, yet if I stirred dirt into the water you would say, "dirty water," but the water is still clear. If we strained the dirt out through a filtration system or allow the dirt to settle, we would again be left with clear water, because water's nature is clear. The same is true for our minds. Our minds are in the nature of clarity and peace, but the delusions are like the dirt in the water. We see an impure mind stirred with delusions of fear, anger, jealousy, depression, greed, and so on, and we relate to the *dirt* as being *who we are*. We will even say in our language *I am angry*, or *I am sick*, but what is really happening is that we have anger arising in us. We have sickness in us. If we were inherently angry we would be angry twenty-four hours a day, seven days a week. The delusion is like the dirt that clouds the clear mind.

What we will be doing within the pages of this book is removing the dirt or purifying (transforming) our minds, so to speak, so we can realize that our minds, like the water, were always clear, peaceful and happy. The proof that our minds are in the nature of peace and clarity is that when a delusion arises within us, such as anger or jealousy, when we remove it or let it pass through us, what we are left with is a peaceful mind.

We can train our minds to relate to the clear, peaceful, unlimited nature of true reality as opposed to the fixed, limited, and delusional minds that we know all too well. We can begin to create the habit for peace instead of continuing to create habits for delusion on an unconscious level.

This is an important concept: the true nature of the world is change, all things in constant flux, limitless opportunities, unbounded potential, yet we often relate to ourselves as fixed and stuck, limited in our potential, a view that inevitably brings about suffering. We want to change, but we don't and so we think we can't change. We feel stuck in unfulfilling ways of being and relate to that fixed self that cannot change. This is only a view, and it can be changed, it's one view in the realm of infinite possibilities we will soon unfold.

I once heard a great analogy that pertains to this perfection. Picture two people talking. When you talk to another and you are being positive—"Oh, I love your hair, how's things?" and so on—the conversation seems to flow. Everything is in perfect order. Yet, as soon as someone berates the other or negative conversation starts to flow—"I hate you, life sucks" and so on—suddenly there seems to be static in the conversation. All is not in perfect order. Yet, beyond the static of delusion it is all still flowing in perfection. We just now are blinded by the static of delusion and so now see imperfection, yet there is perfection even in the seeming imperfection.

All spiritual traditions, religions, sages, and mystics from all walks of life talk of getting back to that peace and clarity, that space of perfection, the changeless in a world of change, whether we label this as *god union* or *heaven* or the many other names it has been given throughout history. There are many words to explain and many paths to get back to where you already are, and as the Buddha taught us, do not believe a word I say, try it and see if it is truth for you. This rule should adhere to any path you choose.

In the coming chapters, we will begin to put all we have been learning here into action. We will learn to become conscious creators of our lives as opposed to bundles of habitual reactions, we will learn how to respond to life instead of unconsciously reacting to all of our lives, and in turn create more peaceful and abundant lives for ourselves and others.

There is nothing wrong with reactions; it is just that currently most of our reactions come out of the limited views of anger, jealousy, greed, and so forth. When we learn to transcend our ignorance, then our reactions come from a place of purity and balance, not ignorance and imbalanced minds.

You may be asking, "Well if we are already pure and perfect beings, then why do I have to *do* anything but live?" To this I would say that you are perfectly correct, no pun intended. Yet we may say this, we may intellectualize this, but we don't realize it. And *living* is something we rarely do. Instead we are caught in a world of surviving. It seems that we have to do a lot of work often to get back to where we already are.

All of the practices and techniques you will be learning will be to help us get back to that perfection. By transforming the beliefs we hold about who we are, we take possession of the keys that open the doors to abundance, love, and joy we all seek. As we begin to realize the truth in small ways in our lives we realize that the key to having everything is by wanting nothing, not becoming a reclusive person who gives everything up, yet giving up the insecure notions that we are not *good enough or worthy enough.* The notion that we are separate from what makes us happy or whatever the view is that keeps us from enjoying and experiencing all of life's wonders in whatever form it may take. We will soon learn that it's in changing our minds that we change our worlds, however we wish to experience this. The irony is that once we shift the mind from one of lack and want to *I am the source of it,* then the belief is that we already have it because there is no insecure *want,* and it naturally flows in. There is a bit of clearing out we have to do before we get there, but alas change is not only possible, it is what's happening on a constant basis: so we will now learn how to direct this change in our lives.

Our Gardens

Allow me to make the analogy of our lives being like a garden. Our lives are born out of the mind that creates them, so really we are talking about the mind here.

It is as if we were standing in a garden full of thistles and thorns and weeds, overgrown and messy. We look over at another garden, and it looks beautiful, nice flowers, neat and orderly. *We need to have words with our gardener,* we think. Then we realize that we are the gardener.

Our minds are the result of the seeds we have planted, and so we begin by simply recognizing the flowers from the weeds. If we don't know which are which, then we are hopeless in trying to create the garden we wish to have. There is nothing wrong with a garden full of weeds, thorns, and thistles if this is what you wish to experience. Yet, if it isn't, then this is where we begin, in the cultivation of mind.

Like a good gardener, we learn to tell which seeds produce a flower or fruit-bearing tree and which produce weeds and plants we do not desire to have in our gardens. We can do this through certain meditation techniques. These will help us (a) to better understand and know the seeds we are planting, (b) to uproot the weeds that we don't wish to be there anymore, and (c) to become conscious observers of the thoughts and emotions in our daily lives. This is meditation in action—our living meditation if you will. Once we see and learn which seeds create which results, we are well on our way to creating the garden we wish to have as opposed to the garden of unconscious seeds mindlessly strewn about.

This is what we are doing here, creating the gardens we wish to experience by cultivating them. The garden is the analogy for our minds, and the fruits and flowers that we reap is the world in which we experience what we have sown.

To create a beautiful garden, we will have to get a little dirty and do a bit of work clearing it out first. The fruits and flowers we reap as a result of becoming a more skillful gardener here will far outweigh the sweat of pulling weeds and uprooting habits that do not suit us. Remember, let's have fun here in every process, joyfully clearing out the garden as well as planting seeds to enjoy abundant fruits and flowers.

CHAPTER 3
MEDITATION

We are what we repeatedly do. Excellence, then, is not an act, but a habit.
~ Aristotle

There are so many stigmas when it comes to meditation. It has been synonymous with religion and spirituality, yet the fact is that anyone can practice meditation without any conflict to their current religion. In fact, some meditators have no particular religion or faith and are atheist or agnostic. Meditation is a science of the mind that goes with any lifestyle. Often when we think of the word *meditation* we think of the statues and pictures we may have seen of ancient masters sitting stoically. We may think that meditation may make us boring and life-less. Yet quite the opposite is true. The fact is that we are meditating all the time, and when we learn to direct our meditations, we actually become more dynamic, lighthearted, and joyful. As we learn to accept ourselves the way we are, we learn to let go and move forward in a pos-itive direction of change within the flow of our lives. Some believe that we need to go off to a secluded area and cut ourselves off from our lives in order to meditate. Although meditation retreats are a great way to deepen your practice, the fact remains that it is best to stay in your life as you practice because life *is* your practice, your training grounds and place of learning. If your house were on fire, you wouldn't go someplace else to put it out would you? Of course not. Meditation is right here, right now, as we learn from the painful situations in our lives as well as the joyous ones, from our successes as well as from our failures. What then is meditation?

The Tibetan word for meditation is *Gom*, which literally translates into "to familiarize." So what we are doing in meditation is attempt-ing to familiarize our minds with their true nature of peace, clari-ty, happiness, joy, abundance, or whatever it is you wish to enrich your life with. I have heard people say, "I can't meditate." Yet we are meditating all the time. Sitting in formal meditation is only one method, as we will see later in this book. The views, or beliefs we gain in life are played in our subconscious over and over twenty-four hours a day, seven days a week, whether we are aware of it or not.

So we are constantly familiarizing our minds with thoughts of lack, insecurity, anger, and so forth. These views lead to our meditating on them incessantly in the unconscious mind. When a situation arises, those meditations, or thoughts, spark an emotion, creating an action, which creates our reality—or often an inaction, our inability to act on something due to fears or anxieties, which also produce results in our lives whether it be lack, missed opportunities, or whatever the situation may be.

Think of your mind as being like a muscle, it can be trained, and we are constantly training it and habituating it on an unconscious level, and now we will learn how to consciously train it.

From a standpoint of creation in our lives, not all our views are disempowering, many bring us strength, wisdom, and abundance. Often our painful views bring us empathy, wisdom, and so on. What we are attempting to do here is go in and cull out or transform the views that are unconsciously bringing us lack, fear, and the like. We will be learning how to be the conscious creators of our lives.

Again, right and wrong are words to explain what is desirable (right), something that creates happiness in our lives and the lives of others, and undesirable (wrong) something that creates an undesirable result or suffering in our lives and the lives of others. *Evil, wrong,* and *bad* are just words: I like to explain it as an ignorance. We all have ignorance in us that causes ourselves and others pain in small and large ways, call it *bad, evil,* or whatever your mind wishes to label it. So we have these wrong views that we can trace back to our childhood or another point in our lives.

Those wrong views from our childhood, and forward from there, lead to wrong meditation (or thinking) consciously and unconsciously. Wrong thinking runs like a tape in our minds, leading to wrong actions, or sometimes inaction. This causes us to freeze up with fear and do nothing: we create undesirable results in our lives as well. So what can we do? Well, we are about to explore a radical system that I believe will surprise you in its results. We just read about the science of meditation and how useful and powerful it can be in our lives—so let us begin there.

Meditations to Help Train the Mind for Success
Two Types of Meditation

Two meditations we will be working with to clear out and ultimately create the gardens we wish to have will help us in two paramount ways. The first will help us simply to stop, and the other will help us see clearly, allowing us to transform impediments to all we wish to experience in our lives. *Wisdom* is another word for seeing clearly. Let us begin by investigating the first meditation in the next few sections. Then we will move onto the second.

The first meditation teaches us a skill that in this modern world is often difficult to cultivate: the simple art of stopping, the *sacred pause*, as Tara Brach puts it. Learning to stop is a prerequisite for creating all that comes next. We are trained to go-go-go in this culture, often even having trouble stopping and resting when we are on vacation. We are constantly distracted with technology, our thoughts, and so on. It's difficult for us to truly stop and relax. In this context we aren't just talking about stopping to take a rest, we are talking about stopping for a moment to allow the mind to reflect when a delusion arises, when a thought triggers an uncomfortable and often painful emotion. Instead of reacting unconsciously, we practice stopping, which is not an easy feat. Think of a time when someone said something that made you angry. Is it easy to just stop and not react? Not likely. Most of the time we unconsciously react to people and situations and therefore we unconsciously create our results and reality. By learning stopping we can begin to bring mindfulness into the situation and become conscious creators of our lives.

What we call an *emotion* is the brain triggering an electrical impulse within the body. Our reactions to emotions are either revolt or grasping. If the emotion is unpleasant, we push it away, pressing it deep down (suppression), which leads to many physical ailments. If the emotion is pleasant we grasp at it or cling to it. We often grasp at painful emotions as well: we feel they will protect us, and the brain, whose main function is to protect us, convinces us to do so like when we are angry. We grasp in several ways. We grasp at these delusions and allow them to take us for a ride. We basically give up our control to them. Anger makes us do and say things we later regret, and so do most delusions. We also grasp in that we buy into the delusion, thinking, *Yes I am an angry person* or *Yes I have a right to be angry at this person*. Although people say and do things that are not always appropriate, we are the boss of our lives. When we practice stopping, we begin to realize that we have the choice in every situation to create the outcome. We say things such as "I am angry" or "I am jealous" or "I am sick." Instead we should say "I have anger" or "I have anger arising in me" or "I have sickness in me."

By relating to the delusion as inherently who we are, we remain stuck and fixed and cannot change. This is not logical and goes against all of the science of who we are. After all, since we are constantly changing, everything we say, do, look at, read or interact with in any way changes us, and we change it as well. Like a river, we are constantly flowing and moving. Since we are not angry twenty-four hours a day seven days a week, this is proof that we are not inherently angry. What happens is that anger arises in us like a wave in the ocean. When someone says or does something or whatever the situation may be, the brain triggers that habit energy: the habit for anger in this situation, and anger arises. So we have a habit to get angry. Our reaction is based on our habits, like the example of two people hearing the same thing: one reacts with a laugh and the other with anger. The difference? Their habits and pre-conditions created by their beliefs or views from past experiences. Anger is a self-pitying and self-righteous emotion that arises when we do not get what we want. When someone does not act the way we wish, or when we don't get some thing or situation that we want. This emotion is cultivated from when we were children and first experienced the pain of not being able to have something that we wanted. It's a childish and immature emotion that we carry with us long into our adulthood and beyond, as are most delusions.

It is important to note that the emotion is arising from a thought, and that thought is arising from a past condition: it has nothing to do with the present condition. Although we relate to it as being the same, in fact we often argue that it is exactly the same, but in reality it is just some fantasy, a lie, a story we have conjured up from some past experience we are projecting onto the present moment. When these emotions arise, we can push them down and suppress them until they go away. Then, however, soon after you may find yourself wondering why you have all these physical ailments: because suppression leads us to lash out someplace else, or project it on someone else, and often it turns to a physical ailment.

If we are not suppressing the emotion, we hop on the wave of emotion (grasp at it) and let it takes us on a wild ride that usually ends up disappointing and causing suffering for others as well as ourselves: we say and do things under the influence of delusion that we regret. Luckily those are not our only options. Another option is to use the negative emotion as an opportunity to learn and change the habit to something more empowering something more of use to the world, our world. The first step then is to simply stop and observe the delusion, without pushing it away or engaging in it. Because when we engage in the delusion when it is strong, it will always convince us that it is right. It will say, for instance: "Yes, you have a right to be angry," and then we engage in anger. It's like a car salesman (nothing against car salesmen, they just do their jobs well, hence the analogy). If you go into the dealership with the intention that you are not buying and engage the salesman, often they are convincing enough, and you walk out with a new car, and then you think, *Darn, how'd he do that? I said I wasn't gonna buy today.* The delusion is very manipulative and convincing, so it is best not to engage in it while it is strong. Instead just allow it to be there without judgment. Just observe it without the need to grasp at it and follow it, without the need to push it down deep and bury it. Allow the pain to be there and know that it, like all things, will pass away. This is where we can begin to develop insight instead of confusion. Let's look at how we can begin to implement this into our lives.

Chapter 4
Stop, Name, and Note: the Power of Acceptance

I am God's Lion, not the lion of passion. The sun is my lord. I have no longing except for the One. When a wind of personal reaction comes, I do not go along with it. There are many winds full of anger, and lust, and greed. They move the rubbish around, but the solid mountain of our true nature stays where it's always been. ~ Rumi

The following are explanations of two very simple steps that can have profound effects on the quality of our lives and those around us.

Step 1: Stopping - We can do this by simply stopping and breathing (we will be learning some basic breathing and writing techniques later in this book that will help us calm emotions and anxieties when they are a bit more powerful and overwhelming).

Simply by staying present, by just stepping back for a moment when anger arises, or whatever it may be, without getting on board the runaway train of the delusion of anger is the first step. We never know where that train will take us, and as we get off we are often upset at our actions. For example if someone says something hurtful to you, and your habit is for anger to arise, then when you hop on that wave of anger it will take you for an often wild ride. You will say things and or do things that later you may regret. Or adversely, you may stuff it down and suppress it and then think: *Oh, why does my back hurt so bad?* Stopping is the first step. The sacred pause, simply observing without engaging in or pushing away the painful emotion is the first step. There are many ways to *stop*, as we will explore, and as always find what works for you.

When we learn to stop we can begin to respond to life as opposed to reacting. We then begin to consciously create our lives. For instance, if someone pinches us, our reaction may be to pinch them back out the reaction of anger, but if we stop, we allow space to think: *Is this what I wish to create here?* Our reactions just cause us to stay locked in an unconscious chain of action–reaction. Yet, if we simply allow ourselves to stop, we bring wisdom to our lives and can create whatever outcome we wish to experience and give to others. It is not easy not to react to delusions such as anger. This is why we will be investigating some great techniques and methods for doing so later in this book.

In any moment, no matter how lost we feel, we can take refuge in presence and love. We need only pause, breathe, and open to the experience of aliveness within us. In that wakeful openness, we come home to the peace and freedom of our natural awareness. ~Tara Brach

Step 2: Acceptance by naming and noting – Accepting where we are and embracing our life in each moment, good or bad, then we can begin to transform it. It is helpful to name the delusion as it arises. In fact this step alone can transform your life. Simply say out loud or inwardly, *anger, jealousy, greed, miserliness, fear* or what ever the emotion may be, calling it what it is without pushing it away or grasping at it. Observe it as it passes through you, accepting it as it is.

I had a situation where someone said something that created a deep well of anger in me. I was about to engage it and say something back, causing a possible World War III cataclysm, but instead I walked away, went into a stairwell in the building where I was, and sat there saying to myself, "Anger, anger, frustration, anger." I allowed it to be there, I accepted the painful emotion that I usually suppressed or engaged, and with time, it slowly began to dissipate, moving through me. We don't scold the emotion and feel bad about the fact that it is there; we accept it without judgment; we observe how it makes us feel and where we feel it. Remember, we are human beings and it is OK to experience delusions and feel pain, allow yourself to be human. Everything is temporary; everything arises and passes away: good states and afflictive states. The fact is that when painful states of being arise, we don't like them; by accepting the pain we decrease them significantly.

There was a study and program done with patients with rheumatoid arthritis where patients were taught basic mindfulness meditation. The results after the program were that each one of them experienced forty to fifty percent less pain when they (a) accepted that they had physical pain and (b) then practiced being in the present moment with it.

What usually happens is that we have the initial pain. Then we create more pain emotionally on top of this because we get angry and frustrated at the fact that we have pain. Simply by accepting the pain as it is, *because* it is—we invite it in, being present with it—and then the pain is reduced and often eliminated in the case of emotional pain.

No one can truly make you angry or sad, only your mind can do this. Others are merely catalysts for this delusion to arise in you. Therefore you hold the power to change this. For example you and I can be standing next to each other and someone can say something, anything. Perhaps I get angry about it, but you think it's funny and laugh. Or perhaps you are neutral, and it doesn't bother you. The same words have been said to both of us, yet there have been two different reactions. I was in the habit of getting angry based on my views developed from the past, which created a habit (a neural pathway in the brain). You, on the other hand, weren't in the habit to react that way in this specific situation. I am not saying that people don't say or do inappropriate things. Yet we can learn to respond to them instead of react. And in this way we easily deter danger or foolishness with a clear mind. It's a mind riddled in delusional anger, jealousy, or what have you, that stays engaged in foolishness and danger. This is the summit of changing our habits, and simply this alone will have a huge impact on your life if practiced.

Naming and noting a delusion is not new, it is an ancient technique that has been used by sages and masters of all walks of life: like the shaman who would create names for the *evil spirits* in the spirit world in order to understand and transform them, we too can create a mythology for our psychology. Like Mara, who—with lust, pride, fear, and so forth—tempted the Buddha under the tree, or Satan, who tempted Jesus, our mythology has the same characters, perhaps just different names. This helps us to see the unseen forces in our lives. What is unseen is feared, and our fears give the unseen strength and power over us. We fear what we can't see and understand.

One of my students once had a fear of taking tests, and so she asked if she could name that specific fear *Charlie*. I told her this was brilliant, that this is exactly what mythology is doing, giving a name and face to the often elusive and fleeting energies that run amuck in our psyches, creating our outer worlds. I told her to invite Charlie in for tea, sit him down and get to know him, and ask why is Charlie afraid. This is a radical concept, it's like inviting our enemies over for dinner, the ones who cause us great pain and suffering. Yet, what happens is that when you get to know the enemy and they know you, soon you are friends and they do not want to harm you anymore. Then you may suggest to them that *perhaps you are best suited for another purpose in my psyche, one that empowers us.* Again, I would recommend that while the delusion has a strong hold, do not engage in it until it has calmed. We do this by stopping and accepting it. Then, when the energy of delusion has passed and doesn't have a hold over us, we can begin to understand it. Only then can we transform it. If we do not understand something, it is nearly impossible to transform it.

The fact is that delusions are rooted in ignorance, they are like children who don't know any better, and so we must be the parents to compassionately teach them that what they are doing is causing pain and suffering. If the child is an angry mess, we do not try to talk to them in that state because a rational conversation will not come from a child that is fuming with rage and tears. We may send them to their rooms and let them calm down first instead of engaging them. We are not trying to get rid of them. This will lead to them lashing out even more. We are transforming them into empowering emotions. We are teaching the child with compassion, changing the habit from one that is destructive to one that is constructive within our lives.

Oftentimes we are just walking down the street or driving to work, and a thought comes up seemingly out of nowhere. Or perhaps it was fed by a stream of thinking about something else. Usually we notice the emotion first, as the thoughts are many and hard to pinpoint. We can be in a great mood, and then it happens: the thought of a person in the past or a situation, whatever it may be, makes the emotions of anger, frustration, or perhaps jealousy come up. Let's say you are walking and a thought about someone or something in the past (possibly the very recent past like a few hours ago) arises, and anger and frustration now come flooding in. Oftentimes we think *Oh no, I shouldn't think like that* or *So and so isn't such a bad person, they're just misunderstood* or whatever. And so we actually start to feel guilty about what we are presently feeling and stuff it down and push it away because we think we shouldn't feel that way. Well guess what? You are feeling it at the present moment. And whether you think it is right or wrong is irrelevant, at this point you must not push it away or grasp at it. Many times we also grasp and follow it and think *I can't believe them, I can't believe they would say that* and so on, and rage and frustration grows in our mind, further strengthening the habit, often when the person isn't even there. And then we walk into the house and give our children an attitude because we are in a deluded mind. And now we are spraying it onto everyone else, and they wonder: *What's wrong with Mom, she's always in a bad mood*—or whatever the situation.

This works very well with addictive cravings as well. In fact when it comes down to it, it is all addiction: we are all addicted to something, be it thoughts, substances, situations, whatever it may be. Often physical addictions such as those to drugs, alcohol and sex, can be very strong—just like the addiction to anger. When these come up, and we are trying not to indulge in said addiction, we often feel guilty, thinking that we are some sort of *bad* person for feeling these cravings or anger or jealousy. The truth is that you are human. It's OK to feel these things. You are not some outcast. We all experience delusion. Even the Buddha himself felt lust and anger and temptation. In that moment you can tell yourself that it is OK to feel this. In fact, in that present moment it's not your fault: it's the beliefs and views from the past that have created this habit. So by accepting it, you allow it to pass through, and with time, as we will see later, you will be able to change the habit.

It takes time to break a habit, so be gentle with yourself. Instead of getting down on yourself and pushing the emotion away and suppressing it, causing you further pain, and instead of engaging in it, which at the time may feel good to do with physical addictions, instead just allow yourself to feel it. You can say internally, *anger, frustration, craving,* as you name it and feel it. Soon it will dissipate, move through you, sometimes longer than sooner, depending on the depth of emotion. But most will pass through you as easily as they came. The key here is not to suppress afflictive emotions and not to get down on yourself for thinking and feeling them. This will perpetuate them and or suppress them, leading to more issues internally and externally. If I tell you not to think about pizza, what pops in your mind? Exactly, so if you try to push it away, it grows stronger. And when you *do* manage to suppress it, it creates physical issues, usually, or comes back stronger and harder or in a different form.

These first two steps, *stopping* and *accepting*, are the foundation for clearing out our gardens. We will soon get into methods of transforming them and creating new gardens with beautiful flowers and fruit-bearing trees. For now just practice stepping back, pausing, breathing, and naming the delusion as it passes through us. We can start with an entire day of *stopping and accepting* before we react to the people and situations of the day. Just taking a simple second or two to recognize what comes up or think about how we are about to respond can begin the habit to do so, and you may find you are more skillful in what you do that day. Perhaps you pick one person for today to practice with. Perhaps that person is someone you often have difficulties with. It could be one of your children. Before reacting, take a moment to stop and reflect on what is arising. This does not have to be a long and weird pause, just a brief moment where you can ask *Is this a beneficial way to react to this?* If not you can skillfully replace it with what will be more beneficial, or say or do nothing at all and wait until you are clear on it to respond, if the situation warrants it.

Acceptance does not mean we become a doormat, and it doesn't mean that we learn to *feel good* all the time. We are grasping and pushing away emotions all the time impeding our natural flow of change. As the Tao puts it, we are blocking the nature of who we are, change, by trying to hold onto something or conversely pushing it away. All things pass away and change, so we surrender or accept the pain and just allow the process of life to move through us.

We can start our day with an intention: *I will welcome all my emotions today and intend to use them as tools to awaken.* This will change our whole outlook and day. By setting this intention in the beginning of the day, you will be ready to learn from your emotions as opposed to fighting them as we usually do, both consciously and unconsciously. So first we have to accept our situations. Then we can deal with them, and with patient acceptance we can transform any situation. This takes a courageous and warrior-like attitude, often because we naturally want to run away from pain and push it away. We feel it threatens our very existence. It's OK to feel what is inside of you. And remember, it's OK to smile, because no matter how difficult the situation, we have the power and wisdom to change it by changing ourselves.

Why do we Fear Delusions?

Delusions are mostly rooted in fear. We often fear and feel bad about the delusions that arise in us. Perhaps we believe that they take us off our path, yet they are part of our path. We should accept them as our teachers: like how a crazy, hyperactive child can teach us patience. And within that mind of patience we can transcend the child. Only when we accept where the child is will we be able to help him or her change. If we are always fighting the child or resisting him or her, then we create opposition, dualism—a war. And in any opposition, each side grows stronger to defeat the other. What we need is unity. We need to sit and understand the child, the delusion, the state of mind, the emotion. And the first step is patient acceptance.

When a painful emotion arises in us, we feel bad that we feel bad. Accepting and embracing the suffering, like reaching out and hugging another person, will begin the healing process. This, coupled with mindful awareness and the techniques we will be learning, will help us greatly in the process of transcendence of our painful emotions and situations in our lives. When destructive habits come up, we can use compassion. We can say, "I see you." Not in a scolding way, just in a mindful way, noting that we know what is going on. We can ask ourselves, *Who am I hanging out with? Who is angry, who is craving? Who is unhappy?*

Remember that the delusion is rooted in ignorance; it is not *who you are*. And as with a child, compassion allows us to heal the damage habit creates. We can learn to sit with the delusion, learning to be fearless. We can name or note the emotion: *Scared, fear, I feel scared, I touch the fear, I see you fear, I recognize you.*

In this way we don't grasp at and follow the fear, thinking this is *who we are* and relating to it, and we don't push it away. Grasping and aversion come in many forms; it is wise to recognize all the faces it takes in your life.

In this way we begin the journey of understanding. When we don't understand something, we are powerless over it. We fear, and anger becomes a defense in all its many forms. When we begin to recognize and understand the habit energy that brings us experiences we wish not to show up in our lives, then we can learn from them and begin to transform them.

Suppression, Physical Pain, and Illness

At the age of sixteen I first threw my back out. It was the most painful experience I have ever had. I was bedridden for a week. It passed many a painkiller and depressed day later, and I was back to normal. Yet this pain would come and go for the next ten years, debilitating me often for weeks. As a young guy, I was upset. I began to surf less, snowboard less, and used general caution in all I did so as to be mindful of my back. Doctors never seemed to be able to heal me. They just offered a temporary fix. They said I had bulging disks in my lower back. By the time I was around twenty-five years of age, I was regularly getting cortisone shots into my spine by a doctor who recommended I get back surgery. This was very upsetting.

One sunny summer day as I lay with my feet elevated onto my mother's couch, flat on the floor in pain on a weekend away from my busy New York City job and life, I looked at the bookshelf and saw a book, "Healing Back Pain," by John E. Sarno. It was very serendipitous, as later I would ask my mother where she got the book, and she had no idea. I will only briefly get into his findings here, yet his popularity and ninety-nine-percent cure rate will allow you to find info on him and his books and lectures all over the Internet.

Dr. Sarno studied psychosomatic medicine and conducted research for decades. He denoted that most back pain, neck pain, irritable bowel syndrome, and a massive list of other ailments, are attributed to suppressed rage, anger, and sadness in our lives. His studies showed that we have a sort of reserve in our minds that we fill up from birth with suppression of rage, anger, sadness, and the like. Our minds can handle a great amount of these suppressions, but as the reserve begins to overflow, this is where the problems start.

From birth we begin filling this reserve, crying for a toy, or we experience a sad or horrific event in our lives and so on. We can't stay sad and angry forever, so at a point we suppress and go on with our lives.

Dr. Sarno's research suggests that when we fill that reserve to the brim (and some fill theirs earlier in life, depending on their lives and some not until later if ever) the brain knows that we can't handle all this emotional turmoil, and so the brain does what it is designed to do: protects us. It protects us by diverting the mental pains that are in the unconscious mind to a physical pain, such as a back pain. This way we are dealing with the physical pain and do not have to ever confront the mental anguish, the great distraction. He calls this TMS (Tension Myositis Syndrome) where the brain sends a signal to the body to cut off a small amount of oxygen to a specific area, which can cause immense pain. When the brain protects, it does so in a primordial way, using fear-based methods.

I was fortunate to be able to see Dr. Sarno, as at the time he was taking patients in New York City, not far from where I was working and living. First he checked my physical body and assured me that this was not a physical problem. He was no crackpot Doctor, he held a degree from Columbia University of Physicians and Surgeons and was both teaching and practicing medicine at New York University's School of Medicine for many decades. Next he assured me that it was normal for people in their early twenties to have degenerated disks, and it's not painful. He told me that a slipped disk and hurt back is extremely hard to accomplish. It can happen in massive car accidents or from falling from a four-story building, but not from picking up the morning paper, as was often my case. The back is one of the strongest parts of the body. He said that the brain is smart. It knows where you will believe an injury. Perhaps you had an accident awhile back, as I had. Whatever the situation, the brain is crafty and will use that as an excuse often to initiate pain. (This is not to say you cannot get a legitimate pain or injury from an accident, but my accident was when I was eleven years old, and at age sixteen I started to feel it.) Whatever the case may be, the brain will use the situation to initiate the pain and diversion process. Sarno says that it is whatever is en vogue. It used to be ulcers, and when we realized that ulcers were stress induced, less people got them and it moved to other ailments. A hundred years ago back pain, carpal tunnel, and things of this nature were very rare. Now, eighty percent of Americans have back pain, and the medical community makes billions from it. We used to type on heavy machines that took a lot more wrist action than now, with no sign of carpal tunnel. It makes one curious. Most doctors are trained only in surgery and chemical medicine, and so they were not being malicious. They just hadn't learned about the mind–body connection. So they never had the opportunity or training to delve into it as deeply and methodically as Dr. Sarno had. Psychosomatic medicine is not good for a pharmaceutical-dominated economy, and when pharmaceutical companies have a hand in writing medical textbooks, well, you do the math.

Long story short: within two weeks I was back-pain free and have been for close to a decade. *How?*, you may ask.

His method is one of education and writing. I made a list of all the painful emotions in my life and situations and began to write about them, allowing them to come to the surface from suppression. He said I didn't have to deal with all of them. If we did, no one would be cured. He said that simply knowing that this is what is causing my back pain and writing heals the back: a combination of knowledge and writing. It was the most liberating experience: I was back surfing, running, snowboarding, jumping off cliffs, you name it.

When I told Dr. Sarno I had been doing much breath meditation, he told me that he had seen many of his patients heal quicker when they do breath meditation in conjunction with the writing. He said it was a form of talking to your higher self, similar to writing.

The techniques outlined in this book works to eliminate pains of a physical nature, yet we go a little deeper into a level of change here. I found that the back pain then moved to knee pain. Dr. Sarno said this is normal, it's called *chasing it out*, so I chased it out using writing. It then created some eczema (a rash on my hands I used to experience in my youth as a child, undoubtedly due to suppression of things I was exposed to as a youth). I chased it out again. When I began applying the techniques I am suggesting here in this book, I realized that it works in much the same way, and for me much better because a more lasting change takes place.

In the next section we will talk about incorporating talking and writing to become our own therapists and uproot views that have created habits that cause us pain and dis-ease. This is not to discount traditional therapy, nor am I a medical doctor. If you have an injury, I implore you to seek medical attention, and if you wish to seek out a doctor or therapist who specializes in what I have just wrote about, you can easily find them. Dr. Sarno has since retired, but his work goes on with many credible and amazing doctors and therapists. I wanted to share my story of what to me was an incredible and simple healing utilizing the mind–body connection. If you research further you will find thousands of other testimonials like this, including those from famous actors, athletes, and many other fields.

CHAPTER 5
BEING OUR OWN THERAPIST, TWO SIMPLE AND EFFECTIVE WAYS TO USE WRITING

I am about to outline two very effective methods that have changed my life and the lives of others in paramount ways. These two methods can be done in as little as five minutes each, or much longer: it really depends on how much time you feel you need to commit to it. Sometimes a minute is enough, and sometimes twenty minutes or more is needed. You will know how long you need when you practice. These two methods parallel the two meditation methods we will be utilizing to consciously create our life. And since we are first discussing stopping and acceptance, I would like to outline these two methods here before we go any further. The first method is basically a method to keep us from (a) engaging in the powerful emotional energies that tend to control us and keep us engaging in actions that produce undesirable results and (b) conversely, from suppressing the emotions so that they grow stronger and take different forms, such as deeper emotional pains and physical pains like back pain, neck pain, digestive issues, and so forth. The second method is all about getting to the root of a situation, emotion, or thought that keeps showing up in our lives. Here we will use writing to get to the root view of why the emotion comes up in the first place. Getting to the root of the habit will give us greater clarity and power to change the results in our lives.

Feel free to make all of this your own and practice however it resonates with you. The way I often use these methods is as follows: since we do not have tons of time to practice often, I write for five to twenty minutes before my meditation in the morning or in the evening. I take my notebook, and if there is a predominant emotion or issue, I write it out to make sure I do not suppress it or grasp at it and let it control me. We will soon see how this works. If I feel clear and calm that day, I will use the second method, where I will look at the patterns that led to an undesirable result or emotion to show up. It is only in this clear mind that we should engage in this second method. Otherwise the emotional energy and delusional mind will be sure to deter us from the wisdom of clear seeing: its function is to protect us, yet protection is the furthest thing from what it is doing. In fact, it is harming us in almost every way possible. So we aren't trying to get rid of these emotions or thoughts. We are not vilifying them with this first method. We are simply allowing them to pass through us as passing storms do: accepting them as we vent to a piece of paper, allowing them to express themselves through a pen as opposed to being expressed by harming others or ourselves with thoughts, words, and actions driven by delusions of anger, fear, jealousy, greed or any of the other delusions we experience day to day.

The First Method
Don't fight it, write it!

Often when a strong emotion is sparked from our incessant thinking (meditations), we fall victim to the emotion and allow it to control us. We are slaves to the emotion, so many times not even realizing the hold it has over us until it is too late. At this point, we usually do either one of the following:

1. We feel the negative emotion of anger, jealousy, greed, fear, or whatever it may be, and we push it away. We stuff it deep down because we think that we shouldn't be feeling this way. We don't want to feel pain, so we suppress it so as not to harm ourselves or others. Often as adults when anger or sadness arises, especially if it's from something we want, we suppress it because we know we can't pout and stomp our feet like little children. Anger arises when attachment doesn't get what it wants. So we suppress the emotion of anger or sadness so we can "act like adults." We are very silly in this rationale of suppression. Even children suppress such emotions because they know they can't stay angry or sad forever; they stuff emotions down and move on to the next distraction. As we have just learned, this is not skillful in any way, and causes more pain in other forms.

2. If we don't suppress the emotion we engage in it. For example, when anger arises in us we say or do things under the influence of anger—either to ourselves or others—that we soon regret. An emotion such as anger is very convincing, masterful at making us self-centered. After all, it is a response from the brain to protect the individual separate self. Sometimes anger will keep

us ignorantly thinking we did the *right thing*. And this sense of self-righteousness can last for days, weeks, or years after we did it, even if we harmed another person. When anger or any afflictive emotion arises, it becomes our master. We are the slaves to follow its every order. It is a tricky thing because we relate to the anger as *who we are* when in fact it's just a passing storm that has hijacked us for a moment.

Writing helps us to stop and learn to create responses in life that skillfully create positive results as opposed to unconscious reactions, which create negative results in our lives. A powerful emotion such as anger can stick with us for a lifetime, often creating destruction, mostly to our own self, internally and externally. When we sit with our pen and pad we can write out how we feel, neither suppressing nor feeling the need to follow the delusion outside of our pads.

Allow yourself to get juicy: often curses and heavy writing ensue, but don't judge the anger or other afflictive emotions. Just allow it to express itself as it will. Remember, you can shred this up right after you write it. It's not about keeping a journal, it's about getting it out of your unconscious mind where it stirs and creates more destruction. It's like if you capture a storm in your house, it will wreak havoc until you let it out. But you don't want to let it out into your neighbor's house. You just want it to go back into the natural elements, releasing it to the sky. This is analogous to what we are doing with writing.

Don't fight the delusional mind and don't engage in it, just write it out until it passes through you. Although I have found that meditation is helpful right after I write, it isn't necessary right after writing. It would be good, however, to meditate within twenty-four hours of writing. Meditation teaches us to let go, and with the writing we will be learning to let go of the storm, not hold onto it. Like all things, it must pass. But we tend to want to hold onto the storm because someplace in our brain we feel it is protecting us from some threatening external force. We don't need anger to stand up for ourselves; we don't need jealousy to keep a lover; we don't need greed to become wealthy, yet we believe we do on some level, and so we allow afflictive emotions to control us time and again.

This is a key factor in becoming the master of our brains as opposed to allowing the brain to rule us and be our master. As we will see in the second method here, the brain is a super valuable organ, and when utilized correctly can be our greatest ally.

We often carry suppressed pain, sadness, and anger from our lives. We can make a list of past and present issues and use these for our writings. Some examples could be worry about the outcome of a project or relationship; anxiousness, anger, or sadness toward a situation concerning ourselves or another person from our past or present; guilt on its many levels; and much more.

Make your list. Don't hold back. I have found that the one thing we avoid most writing about is usually the one we should start with. You may find in time you lighten up, anxieties begin to lessen (as much of our anxiety is caused by our suppressed emotions). You might even see physical pains begin to disappear. Remember this is not by any means a substitute for seeking medical attention or therapy when needed. It is, however, a valuable tool to use in your everyday life that can transform your physical and mental disposition and relationships with others in wonderful ways.

A final note on this first type of writing: as you write or verbalize, you may find that you diffuse a negative view from the past with clarity and wisdom. For example you may be writing about an insecurity or feeling of inferiority in the area of your career, but then begin to realize that you are currently doing very well and that many actually look to you as an authority in your work. What happens often is that when we diffuse the negative and wrong view from the past with our writing, we begin to bring insight into the situation. Perhaps we were the youngest and were never looked at with authority. Thus, we feel insecurity. This causes us pain. We realize, however, that we are actually doing well. We are very capable at what we do. There is no reason to feel insecure in our position. This is just one example. Everyone's process will be different.

Allow positive thoughts to infuse the brain in whatever form they take. Those positive thoughts will actually begin to change the neural structure and habits of the brain. Before they had been about the negative view you once held about a past that doesn't even exist. But your thoughts shift to the reality that you are capable of anything you wish to put your mind to. You can bring your mind back to these positive thoughts when you find yourself dwelling on the negative view.

This brings us to the second method of writing, which is designed to bring that wisdom in deeper for a lasting change. Remember the brain is changing all the time. Neuroplasticity is the brain's capability to change and learn. And so what we are doing is consciously and mindfully directing change to more empowering habits in our lives.

The Second Method
Root Writing

Nothing in life is to be feared, it is only to be understood. Now is the time to understand more, so that we may fear less. ~ Marie Curie

When you sit to write and don't feel particularly compelled or don't have a dominating emotional feeling to write about, if you feel calm and clear, this is a great time to utilize *root writing*: to look at your patterns now with clarity.

Often when our lives are in chaos or painful emotions are present, we practice these methods to alleviate them. Yet, it is very powerful to practice these with a clear mind when things are going well: this is when the real deep work will happen. In fact, some of the biggest insights will come from this clear sense of being. It is in this clear space that we can create and enforce empowering habits of mind and easily uproot ignorant views.

Now we begin to unpack the lies, get down to the view that causes the final results. As an author I love to use writing as a method to do this, yet we can also talk it out with ourselves, as well as use the companioned *laboratory meditation* that we will soon be learning to get deep with it once we are in a peaceful place. As we sit with a somewhat peaceful mind, we can use writing to get to the root of an issue we have been noticing in our lives. We may think that we have already gotten to the root of it, but perhaps we only found one part of the root. Try to trace the delusion back to see where the view started. This can be a very painful process sometimes, but I assure you it is one of great liberation. We can also do this through contemplation and talking it out with ourselves. I've gone for bike rides in the woods alone and talked out loud to myself and have found it very effective and transformative. Talk therapy with a professional is useful in this respect. Often when we talk to a therapist he or she can help us to better understand and get to the root of our delusions and habits. This method is not meant to deter you from professional therapy if you are doing or considering that, it is just another method to use in being your own therapist in respects to changing habits. Try all these self-therapeutic methods and see what works best for you.

Once we have exposed the root, the why, the view, we now have a deeper understanding of why we react the way we do in certain situations, even when the reasons are not even close to the situation at hand. An episode in our childhood could affect something totally different in our adulthood, but connect the dots and you will see the correlation. Be gentle on yourself, even a small amount of clarity is better than no clarity, and often that small dot of clarity allows us to open up in time. This is where we begin to truly heal and change the habits that do not suit us anymore.

Use your intellectual mind; this is a cognitive process; we think about it. Now that our minds are more refined and focused, we are more capable to use analysis to trigger insight. When we gain insight, we then hold it with our concentration. We can drop the analysis here and just hold the feeling of it. When it goes away, you can go back to the analysis and find that feeling again and hold it. This can be a writing meditation. We will now have deep understanding, and this is the platform for changing. We cannot change that which we do not understand. Ignorance renders us powerless. Understanding renders us powerful and able to create anything we wish.

Insight is the light of wisdom we need to clean the garden strewn with thorns and thistles if we wish to create a garden of flowers and fruit-bearing trees or whatever you wish to create in that garden. It's up to you.

You can start with a result and trace it back to the root (the beliefs that created the habits of action time and again) or ask a question, *Why am I so anxious about such and such?* or *Why do I keep choosing the same destructive relationships?* You can write these questions in your notebook and start there, or verbalize it.

I have found different things work at different times. Sometimes I want to write up a storm. Other times I want to go for a secluded walk and talk it out with myself. Sometimes with very difficult situations it is helpful to ask for clarity. When you ask for clarity you are asking your *higher self*, which is tapped into the clear resources and answers residing above the self-centered ego self that is often veiled in confused vision. When you ask for clarity you begin to tap into the all-knowing, whatever that means to you in your belief system. Some call on God, Buddha, Jesus, Muhammad, the Universe, The Source, The Higher Self, or whatever you wish to label it. This can be very helpful. This isn't always necessary, but sometimes when we are in the midst of a great storm, it is comforting to take refuge in however we label and envision the all-knowing field. And when we feel safe, we allow ourselves to open up more, again this is a psychological practice.

When you sit to write, be free and uninhibited. Don't worry that someone may read what you've written. Tear it up as soon as you are done if you like. I know one woman who washes her writings in water. For her, the water symbolizes cleansing. So it's a psychological process for her. Also, the words get washed away so no one can ever read them.

I have burned the papers afterward. On several occasions I have taken all my writings of this sort and burned them on a full moon, allowing that energy to purify them. The full moon is a time where our subconscious comes to the surface, so it's a good time to work on deeper issues. This is why many get loony during the full moon. The more we suppress deeply, the more comes up, especially during the full moon. This is where the word lunatic comes from (root word *luna* meaning "moon").

Remember, all rituals and ceremony are meant to change our psychological mind. So make your own ceremony that resonates with you if you wish. This is not some mystical practice. It's one of changing our mind, creating psychological change for empowerment in our lives. As for our writing, I again encourage you to be uninhibited. Draw pictures if you need to, scribble, write big, small, sloppy, fast or slow, whatever works for you. This is true for both methods of writing.

Sometimes we keep hacking at the weed, and it keeps growing back. No worries. Eventually we will get to the root—so hack away. If you don't get to the root right away, that's fine. There are often layers here to peel away, but keep hacking away at the weed, and eventually you will reveal the root.

When we do get to the root, we can stop writing. When we have that *aha* moment, even if it's only a little insight, we can stop and seal it in. I would suggest that sometime soon, in the next day or so, that you recall the root, that *aha*, and just hold that feeling in your mind to lock it in. When we are writing or talking or whatever method we use we will often get to the *aha* moment. It will open up to us, and you will know what I mean when it happens. This is the point that we expose those wrong views that we relate to and realize that they are just fantastic tales we have created and that we don't have to be held prisoner by them. That is when we want to just hold that in meditation to lock in our understanding of why. We can hold that in our minds for a moment and then just go into that clear space of meditation. Just being in that clear space will seal in the realization. Now that we have that clear space, we are able to fill it with whatever positive and empowering views we wish to. When we begin to create more positive minds in our life, we are actually balancing the neurological imbalances that negative minds create in us.

If you don't get to the *aha* moment and if you are still confused and unclear, this is OK too. Just let it go and meditate. Within that space you will begin to heal, and with time (all in proper time), your intention to understand it will allow you to because you have planted a seed to create understanding and wisdom (seeing clearly).

Once we have the *aha* moment we hold it in meditation. When we lose it, we seek it again with the analytical mind. Then, when we find the aha we hold it again. Hold it for a while to let it seep in. The brain will try to make you forget this insight, so the seeking and holding will often need to be done a few times, being steadfast in your resolve in this method.

Once we have gained an understanding of why we act or create certain situations in our lives, we can ask ourselves, *Who is seeking validation?* or *Who is getting angry?* or *Who fears such and such?* Asking these question we realize that it is just a view based on a past that we currently are not.

We bring to mind that as we are sitting here there is no danger, and so we can let it go and just breathe. We are dismantling the delusions here, the grand fantasies and stories our brains tell us that we believe.

We sort of argue with the delusions and explain to them how they are seeing the situation wrong. We see that although a situation may exist—we may have been harmed or fear some harm—yet we are creating all these layers in a situation that doesn't actually exist. Most likely these afflictive thoughts are based on past conditioning and fears. We bring wisdom and clarity into the situation. Once we get to that calm, clear space, we can just abide there in the absence of our delusion, now knowing the root and the lies that created it.

In short, we can sum up our process here as follows:

We learn to first stop and accept the painful emotions, allowing them to pass. Next we understand why the emotion is coming up, gaining some insight into it. When we understand the view that is creating this, we change by seeing it clearly and bringing wisdom and truth into the lies we have been believing based on past experience that mostly do not exist anymore. When we are in that clear space, we can replace it with a positive thought or way of being. Stop and Accept, Understand, Replace. Simple system, and the more we do this, the more we change the habits of mind to ones that empower us to bring more joy, abundance, and love to the world.

You can use these steps here for *root writing* as well as a meditation. We will soon learn a formal sitting meditation that this system can be incorporated into called *the laboratory meditation*.

Simple tips on *root writing*:

1. Analyze until the insight comes.

2. Hold the insight single-pointedly until you lose it.

3. Analyze again until another insight comes—the feeling of *Oh I get it! I see why I do or act this way* (whatever the situation may be).

4. Hold the insight again.

CHAPTER 6
BREATHE: THE POWER OF BREATH MEDITATION

A basic yet powerful meditation that not only teaches us stopping and letting go but also trains the mind in concentration is simply to focus on your breath. Concentration meditation helps settle the busy mind, which creates our uneasiness and inability to be content in the present moment. The mind is in a constant state of distraction due to thoughts from the past or about the future.

Learning to direct your attention is a very powerful way to reshape your brain and mind. When the mind is focused, we can begin to see our emotions, or else they seem like a mish-mosh of feelings that we can't often pinpoint, and we find ourselves drowning in them. Our modern world is wrought with distractions. As a result, we are more easily trained by the commercialism that plagues our world and thrives on distraction and attention deficit. When we learn to control our attention more, we become more mindful and more able to create our lives to conform to our true needs, rather than to how others wish us to live, caught in a world that dictates what to buy, what to be, and so forth.

Many masters throughout history have realized the value of a steady, calm mind from Jesus, Pythagoras and Einstein to Patanjali, Buddha, and Lao Tzu. Just ask any master athlete and he or she will tell you that a calm and focused mind is key to his or her success. In fact, a focused mind gives us a leg up in anything we do. All masters realized that in changing your mind you change your world. And in the same manner that one learns mathematics, there are levels of learning. You don't jump to calculus before you learn addition. So, breath meditation and other forms of concentration meditation such as *tritak* (where you focus on an object), or focusing on a word or mantra, are the fundamental mindfulness meditations that like addition in mathematics, are used to further all other levels of meditation.

There is intelligence in the breath. When we surrender to it, knowing where we hurt, the body and mind heals itself. Our bodies and minds have an amazing ability to heal; all we need do is rest peacefully. Often when we get sick, we get into a frenzy. *Should I go to the doctor? Should*

I stay home from work? Where's my medicine? Why's this happening to me now? Thoughts disturb our peace and impede our healing. When an animal gets sick it goes off to a quiet place and doesn't do anything but rest. As a result, it will usually heal twice as fast as we do. It's because the animal is in that silence, in the stillness of resting, and in that surrender, the mind and body heal. This is why we sleep every night. Sleep is the natural repairing phase of the body and mind. Unfortunately many of us do not get enough sleep, and the sleep we do get is often disturbed by an active mind.

It is said that Jesus Christ was a master healer. He was said to be able to make the blind see. He could heal lepers as well as a vast array of physical ailments. He could release demons (delusions) from the minds of man. Jesus said that it was not he who healed but the almighty power, the impenetrable field of love that he was able to access. It is my belief that Jesus was an enlightened being, one who had achieved Christ consciousness like the Buddha, one who was awake. In this state he is a clear channel, a vessel for the perfection of love and joy to heal through him merely by raising his hand. We all have the potential to heal ourselves and in effect others, by obtaining that peace and clarity that is the true nature of who we are. We may not be able to access it yet indefinitely at this point of our lives, as Jesus and Buddha had, but we can access it at any moment we stop and breathe. Allowing the incessant thoughts of future and past worry to subside, we open the channel for healing and transformation. When we focus on the breath, we are beginning to subdue the constant chatter that clouds our minds.

The kingdom of God is within you. ~ Jesus (Luke 17:21)

The benefits of breath meditation are many. The short-term benefits are that we feel more peaceful and relaxed, gain more clarity and more control, and become less neurotic. The long-term benefits are that we familiarize our minds with peace, creating the habit for peace, the peace that you already have within you. Breath meditation helps us reconnect with the peace that is already within us, allowing us to come back to the clarity and wisdom and joy that are within us in immeasurable amounts. The fact is that this can be done by anyone and is a prerequisite to begin the work of developing insight and lasting transformation.

Basic Breath Meditation

In breath meditation we simply sit in a comfortable cross-legged position or in a chair with hands in any symmetrical pose you like. If you have a meditation practice, then do whatever you normally do, or what feels comfortable. If you normally place your hands on your lap then by all means do so. I suggest you sit symmetrically as to have balanced energy, when the body is balanced we more easily surrender and relax. Placing the hands in the same position every time we meditate acts as a hypnotic suggestion, like going to sleep every night at the same time, soon your body knows when you come into this position, *time to meditate* and drops down easier with time, so like every action we take, we are creating a habit.

All you are doing here is observing the breath, not trying to control it, simply observing the sensation of breath as it moves in and out of the nostrils. This sounds easier than it is. Our minds will inevitably wander; we have monkey minds that run incessantly from thought to thought all day like a wild horse. With consistency and practice (even only 5 minutes a day!) we begin to be able to focus on the breath for longer intervals without thought disruption. When a thought arises you simply recognize it then bring your awareness back to the breath. We do not push the thought away, because it will only grow stronger and do not grasp at it and follow it. Simply notice it and bring your awareness back to the breath. Remember thoughts are not the enemy, we can notice them like passing clouds in the sky and gently bring our awareness back to the sensation of breath at the tip of the nose. Be gentle at first, in the beginning if you have to bring your awareness back to the breath 50 times in a minute, that's a good meditation. It is important to maintain a passive attitude and not judge yourself or the thoughts for arising, simply recognize them and bring your awareness back to the breath.

With patience and consistency you will find this practice to be transforming. Remember to have fun with it, bring joy into the practice, be gentle on yourself, it's not a race or contest to be judged, yet a simple tool to relax and gain some clarity away from the mundane millings of the daily brain.

Here is a good formula for this mediation

1. Sit in a comfortable position. Relax the jaw, neck shoulders and brain (scan the body and relax it accordingly)

2. Bring awareness to the breath.

3. If it is easier, on the exhalation mentally repeat a word such as *peace, love, relax, surrender* or anything you may resonate with in the moment.

Breath Meditation to Practice Observing Mind and Emotions

Everything arises and passes away, and that passing is peace. ~Buddha

I've had students come to me after doing basic breath meditation for a little while and say, "I think my mind is getting crazier, not more peaceful." I tell them that what is happening is that they are just seeing how the mind is all the time, beyond the distractions they create. When we begin to sit with the mind for a bit, we see that the mind is usually buzzing incessantly. By seeing the mind for what it is, we can begin to calm it, so no worries if you realized—thought after thought, emotion upon emotion—it's just the habit we are currently in. It is what the brain does, but alas we can change if we wish to, gradually settling the mind and increasing our clarity and well-being.

Allow me to elaborate a bit here on the previous meditation. Remember to take what works for you and make this all your own. Have fun with it and note the effects it has on you. There really is no right or wrong way to meditate. So relax and don't be too serious. If you are bringing your awareness back to the breath or word or object, you can practice this with much success.

This is breath meditation, the fundamental meditation that many masters have taught throughout history. These are the basics we can practice every day for as little as five minutes or as much as an hour or more. (I advise you start with five or ten minutes and build on your successes). This meditation is intended to rest the primordial monkey minds that are thrown from one thought to another, seldom resting. Even in sleep we are doing this, which is why many wake up from hours of rest feeling tired. This meditation is designed to slow the mind down.

I remember when I first came to meditation of this sort, I thought, being a writer, that I need all of those thoughts, they are what makes me creative. I was sorely wrong, in fact the incessant thoughts impeded my creativity and clouded my mind, in the calm space of my mind is where the real gold exists, the real art.

As explained previously, we begin by sitting in a relaxed, straight posture, bringing our attention to the breath. Focus on the sensation right at the nostrils as the breath comes in and out. If you are feeling agitated or a little excited, focus on the rise and fall of your belly. In any case, bring about twenty-five percent of your attention to the breath and let the rest just be spacious. When a thought arises, don't suppress it by pushing it away, don't follow it and feed it by entertaining it either. Simply be aware that you are thinking. You can even say in your mind "thought" and then bring your attention back to your breath without any further self-commentary. This is a practice of training the mind in single-pointed meditation. Don't be discouraged if you notice the mind keeps wandering to thoughts and emotions. This is the practice: the mind wanders and we bring it back. This is all we are doing at this point. When our minds are free, without the shackles of our grasping and pushing away, then it is free to come and go like a flowing river. In this practice we begin to liberate the mind and let it naturally flow. If in the beginning, if it helps you focus, you can count your outgoing breaths, from one to ten, then start over and count again. Sometimes counting to five, inhaling, and then exhaling works well. Focusing on the counting helps stabilize the mind. Even just saying, mentally, "in" on the inhalation and "out" on the exhalation works well too. Some find it effective to repeat a word on the exhalation, as I previously noted, saying "peace, love, relax" or any word or phrase you wish. Experiment and see what resonates with you. Once you have stabilized, you can stop the counting or words and focus only on the breath in a relaxed way, consciously observing your inhalation and exhalation. Keep being aware as thoughts arise, then return the mind to the breath. During your meditation sitting times, this may be as far as you get, and this is very good. As I said before, if you have to bring your awareness back to your breath fifty times in a minute, this is a good meditation.

Overtime your mind will begin to calm, and you will have more gaps between thoughts to abide in the calm awareness. Every day will be different, depending on the mind you sit with. When you find yourself in the gap between thoughts, simply relax in that gap, and with practice this gap will become longer and longer as you practice abiding in this bliss. You will begin to be less compelled by your thoughts. You won't cling to them out of habit as you once did. They will lose the power to control you, and you will begin to become the master of your thoughts and mind as opposed to a slave to them.

When we sit in meditation, the mind wanders to things we think we should be doing or thinking. Yet, when we stay with our meditation for our allotted time, we are training ourselves to concentrate better and to not follow the demands of the brain. As I sit on my couch for my morning meditation of twenty minutes, my mind thinks of all the things I should be doing: *I don't have time to meditate for twenty minutes we have important things to do*, it thinks. That is fine because instead of breaking my meditation and following the thoughts, I let them go and I bring my awareness back to the breath. How you do anything is how you do everything, and so this empowering habit will bleed over into all you do. For example, while I sit down to write, the compulsion to check my e-mail or update my Facebook or text or call someone or wherever the mind tries to take me is still there often. Yet I bring my awareness back to my writing and thus complete the task I set out to do more efficiently and with better focus. My brief meditations in the morning help me to focus and concentrate, making me more effective in all I do. This *meditation break*, the time between meditations, is very important. Formal sitting meditation is just a training ground for our lives. However, we can now bring the training into the field and make use of it. With time, it just becomes an empowering habit.

In a culture riddled with Attention Deficit Disorder, this is a great tool to help combat distraction. We can practice bringing our awareness back to a book if we are reading, back to washing the dishes. If we are driving and our mind is drifting off, we can bring it back to the road, to the present moment, we will be doing the world a service as there will be less accidents if we are more mindful. We can practice being truly present when talking to someone, we can listen deeply to what they are saying and bring our awareness to them when we find the mind drifts off. This is our meditation in action. Sitting meditation is just one way to meditate, yet we can practice all day and as a result enjoy our days more deeply with mindfulness. As we change our habits, we are also better role models to our children. The fact is that our children are often a reflection of the habits we instill in them. A parent is a god to a child, and so they emulate what we do on a physical and energetic level. The more empowering habits we create for ourselves, the more empowering habits we project into the world. It is in changing our minds, changing ourselves, that we change the world around us. As Gandhi said, "We must be the change we wish to see in the world."

In meditation, when you begin to come into that gap or spaciousness of your true nature, you can drop all the focus of meditation, surrender to it, and your mind will merge with this space. Just relax in that space and allow the natural clarity to come forth. When again you find the mind drifting off to thoughts, bring it back to the breath. The breath is always there to keep you in the present moment. The breath is always in the present moment. Once you again find that peaceful space within, simply rest in this space again; the experiences will be profound at times and subtle at others. Do not attach or cling to these experiences, as they will vary every time you sit. Surrender is the key here. Have fun and experiment with this, but most importantly, do it with consistency. Even five minutes a day can have profound, long- and short-term effects on your mind and body.

CHAPTER 7
A MATTER OF HEART

When I first began teaching, I had a friend and student named Edward who had a life-threatening heart condition. Ed was on about five different medications for his heart and blood pressure. I had taught him a simple meditation that he later made his own. He would sit and do some basic breathing and then he would either focus on his breath or a word.

Edward was very visual, however, so I encouraged him to use visuals in his meditation. Often the word would be *peace* or *wisdom* or whatever he felt he needed that day. We made a commitment to each other that we would mediate every day for ten minutes, for the next thirty days. Using the honor system, we agreed that if one of us faltered he would have to pay the other a hundred dollars. We made the stakes interesting.

The reason I told him thirty days was because I knew that was a rough time frame to create a new habit, and so after the thirty days, only four short weeks later, a few very interesting things occurred in his life. He said he began waking up and wanting to meditate because he not only created the habit for it but he did so joyfully. He looked forward to his daily meditation, even for only ten minutes. Doing it with joy is very important: it keeps us doing whatever we commit to doing. If we are not bringing joy to everything we do, then what's the point?

Ed later told me that his meditations added clarity to his day. When he would use meditation to breathe in love, joy, peace, and abundance, he would set this intention for his day and reported that his days seemed to *flow* more easily. This little experiment also shocked his doctor. After thirty days, Ed now was taking only two of his five prescribed medications. To his doctor's amazement, his blood pressure was stabilized and his heart was healthy. He soon went down to one medication for the elasticity of his aorta (a precautionary medication). In only ten minutes a day, Ed began to transform his life in ways he hadn't even expected.

Consistency in our practice will lead to wonderful results. Everyone's results will be different in some respect, but the peace we all gain is a constant. Patience and persistence is key in this game. Maybe you too can find a buddy to do this with. Take the 30-day Challenge: start with just five minutes a day. You never know what will happen until you try.

Clean Body, Dirty Mind

There seems to be an excuse in meditation that I myself have not been exempt from at times in my life. We are too busy to meditate. Our lives are hectic schedules of get up and go, and the last thing we need is another thing added to it, right? Wrong. Meditation will serve only to organize and settle the crazy lives we lead. When we wake up, we wouldn't run off to work without bathing and clothing ourselves (most of us anyway). We wouldn't run out of the house half clothed and unclean because we didn't have time to dress properly: running off to catch the train in a suite shirt and our boxer shorts would be a funny scene.

What we don't do is clean our minds. We wake up, and we usually do the opposite. We hear the alarm and think, *Oh here we go again, I'm still here*, and the delusions begin to come in: we think of a particular person we may have to see that we wished we didn't or all of the tasks we have to do that day. The mind goes in all directions. We even fuel ourselves with caffeine, read or watch the news, and busy our minds further. In essence, we are dirtying our minds.

If we take even five minutes, yes only five minutes, to sit and clear our minds with a bit of breath mediation, it can have a profound result on our days. Karma is simply Sanskrit for *action*. Everything we do, think and say is a karma. If we get out of bed and stub our toe, the whole day seems to follow that action: we spill our coffee, miss the bus, we start the ball rolling and don't take a minute to stop. If we simply stop to breathe a moment and clear the mind, we break that chain of action, cause and effect, by bringing in the peace or rather by attuning to the peace that is already there. We can even add abundance, peace, joy, and love by bringing these minds to our practice, if we wish, setting that intention up for the day.

Marcus Aurelius said, "Our life is what our thoughts make it." Our intentions are often not our own: they are usually a result of reactions to something that is coming from outside of us, like a stubbed toe. So why not go inside and reset the intention with skill and awareness? Go ahead, try it now, just for a minute.

CHAPTER 8
JUST BREATHE

When pondered, the simple act of breathing is amazing. Each breath brings in life and regeneration and expels things that attempt to harm us. Many people did not wake up with breath today and sadly many others struggle simply to breathe. In this knowledge we can generate appreciation for the simple faculty of breath.

Two-time Nobel Prize winner Dr. Otto Warburg revealed to the world that the cause of most disease is lack of sufficient oxygen in the body. This is in part due to poor breathing habits. The fact is that most of us do not breathe properly, and a big reason for this is because we are caught in the habit of shallow breathing due to a brain caught in fight or flight most of the day. Just bringing our awareness to the breath is the first step in proper breathing. When we breathe we should breathe deeply into the belly, allowing the abdomen to rise and as we exhale to come back in. Just doing this for a few breaths you will notice change occur.

Our breath is in accordance with our physical disposition at the time. For example, when anxiety arises we have a shallow, quicker breath. Many of my students have come to me with anxiety, and I have had many bouts with the oppression that anxiety brings about at different points in my life. It can feel as though you are drowning, and often the impotence to do anything about it can be devastating and depressing. By altering our breath, we alter our physical body and disposition. The breath is the bridge between the mind and the body. In yoga we use *pranayama* (breath techniques). *Prana* is the life force, directly linked to the breath, and *yama* means "control of," or "drawing out." So you are drawing out the life force and learning proper control of breath to change the body and mind. As you develop into higher levels of practice, pranayama becomes a larger part of the practice. We will get more into this in a moment, but first the anxiety.

I discovered in my practice and many years of study in yoga and eastern philosophy that breath is the cornerstone of it all. When the breath is steady, the mind is steady and the body follows suite. When the breath is disturbed, so is the mind, and then the body. And so I discovered a breathing pattern that quickly offset my anxiety and everyone I have taught has used it with many thanks. The pattern is this, breathe in to a count of four, hold the breath to a count of two, then exhale to a count of seven: a 4:2:7 ratio. A few rounds of this will calm anxiety. I have used it when I wake up in the middle of the night to fall back asleep or just calm myself if I am feeling overly excited.

The ancient yogis developed many breathing techniques for the purpose of getting into deep mediation. Often our minds go from dull to excited and very rarely are they in the middle ground where wellness resides. This is the perfect place to be for deep meditation. Too agitated, and the mind is caught in distraction and busyness. Too dull, and we can fall asleep or just not feel motivated to even practice. Below you will find a chart that maps out three different results of breathing. The first is calming. If you find you sit in meditation or in life and need to calm to get to the middle ground, use these. If you find you are very dull or tired, there are ratios for energy to lift the dullness. And if you feel imbalanced, there are ones to balance. So energizing, calming, and balancing. Play around with these, see which ones work for you, which ones you like, and add them to your toolbox.

Result	Inhale	Hold	Exhale	Hold
Calming	6	1	8	4
Calming	6	1	10	1
Calming	4	1	12	1
Calming	4	1	8	4
Energize	6	4	6	1
Energize	6	6	6	1
Balancing	6	2	6	2
Balancing	8	1	8	1

Bring It Back to the Breath

We breathe all day, yet we rarely are even aware of it. This is the involuntary action that keeps us alive on this Earth. We do not have to sit in mediation to breathe skillfully; we can do this all day. When we find ourselves getting stressed out or angry, we can just stop and breathe, even for a few seconds. We can bring our awareness back to the breath all day long, breaking the cycle of habit that keeps us stressed out, angry, frustrated, or whatever our path to delusion may be. As we do this, we are creating a new habit for peace and relaxation. Again, be gentle with yourself and have the resolve to be consistent.

Try it now. Just sit and become mindful of your breath or try one of the ratios we've just learned. We can begin to appreciate the breath, a faculty that often goes overlooked until we lose it. When I find myself just sitting for a second anywhere I just relax my body and breathe. Even doing this for ten seconds you find tension you were not even aware of.

When I lived in the city full time, I would do this anytime I came to sit on the subway. This creates the habit to do this all day, and soon you are just relaxed and calm, and your body naturally relaxes as a result of formulating a new habit. You are now strengthening your immune system and nervous system, and you loosen up and just simply enjoy.

Remember, we can practice meditating all day. In fact we do just that without even realizing it. The unconscious mind is milling meditations all day. We can't expect to have a mind like a wild stallion all day, grasping and pushing things away in a crazy speed of mind, then think that when we sit down in formal meditation for five minutes the mind will somehow just stop and calm, that somehow we can wave our hand and the stallion will just heed. We can train our minds all day, when we find ourselves getting anxious, angry, frustrated, or whatever the mind is that arises, we can bring our awareness back to the breath and just relax, being mindful of where and who we are.

Just try this right now: bring your awareness back to the breath and relax the body. Perhaps your shoulders are tight or you are clenching your teeth. When we bring awareness to the present we can consciously relax. The more we do this, the more we develop a habit for relaxation and peace and the more we will break the habits of where our minds go automatically in certain situations. We have the choice if we are conscious. With mindfulness, we become conscious creators. Do this while driving, reading, working, or wherever. Just take a minute out to breathe, relax, and just be present in the moment. Whatever you may be doing, even a few seconds can shift your entire energy.

Being aware and mindful of your surroundings, truly being present in the moment works well to combat agitated minds and creates greater awareness of peace. Just take a moment to bring your awareness completely into the present moment. Bring your attention to the room, or wherever you are, completely in the present moment. Colors will seem brighter. Things that seemed fearful or daunting seem to dissipate because in this moment everything is all right. And if it isn't, if there is a threat, being present will make us more skillful to get out of the situation so it's a win-win.

The mind is usually riddled with thoughts of the future and the past. This is a weak primordial fight-or-flight mind, yet the mind that is enriched in the present moment is a mind that is clear and present and strong and able to tackle anything.

When I do this practice, I notice I often smile and sometimes even begin to laugh a bit because what happens is that we tap into that joy that is right there in front of us in this present moment, the joy that is veiled by a mind caught in future or past. And so we can use the breath to be our guide. It is always in the present moment. There is intelligence in the breath. It knows when to begin your life here on Earth and knows when to take your physical body out of it. Allow yourself to tap into that intelligence by being present.

Often we do not appreciate the breath until we lose it. I remember one time when I was body boarding during a storm. The waves were rough and very big and I was hit hard by a large wave that plunged me deep to the bottom of the ocean floor. As I held my board, it propelled me to the surface. But before I could take a breath, I was again hit by another massive wave, smacking me deep down. At this point I needed breath. I almost panicked. But being somewhat experienced, I calmed myself, knowing that it is the panic that drowns people. They panic and breathe in water. "I'll be at the surface in seconds," I told myself, and just as I was to break the surface another massive wave plunged me deep to the ocean floor, again before I could take a breath. This time I thought I was finished and in fact remember almost coming to terms with it. *I am going to die today,* I thought, and I surrendered to something I had absolutely no control over. Still holding my foam body board, I was propelled upward and finally I broke the surface, gasping a large breath before hightailing it back to shore.

I sat and watched the ferocious sea as I breathed and laughed. I think onlookers thought I was a bit mad. I remember appreciating my breath. It was as if I were breathing in gold or something. It was so precious to me! The world smelled sweeter, seemed brighter.

Many did not wake up with breath today, and many others struggle simply to breathe. So allow yourself to generate gratitude for this simple faculty of breath that draws in life with each inhalation. Bring your awareness to your breath and consciously relax all day, creating a new habit, in time, for peace and clarity. This alone can have life-changing effects on you, but remember, to create a new habit you must practice consistency and patience, and soon it becomes who you are. We are practicing all the time with the habits we picked up unconsciously, habits that bring us pain, tension, and other undesirable results. So why not begin to create conscious habits of peace and empowerment in our lives? It is your choice. You are the boss. As Johann Von Goethe said, "Choose wisely, your choice is brief yet endless."

CHAPTER 9
EVERYTHING IS ENERGY

Energy cannot be created or destroyed, it can only be changed from one form to another. ~ Albert Einstein

One of the most basic laws of science is the *Law of the Conservation of Energy* or *The Law of Thermodynamics,* which states that *Energy cannot be created or destroyed, it can only be changed from one form to another.* It is helpful to realize before we go on that everything is energy: a rock, a piece of bread, a table. Every part of the human body is energy as well: our hair and skin and our thoughts and emotions.

What we are beginning to do, and about to discuss in the next section, is work with emotional energy and thought energy. Although I make the analogy of *Our Garden* and *pulling the weeds,* what we are actually doing is transforming the energy from negative to positive. We are changing it from one form to another. In essence, the analogy of weeding a garden is correct, because just like pulling the weeds from your garden to make way for new seeds and growth, those weeds will not just go away. We can put those weeds in the compost pile where they will break down and become nutritious soil with which we fertilize our new garden. So they are changing form as everything does at some point, whether a human body that changes constantly or a rock that slowly decomposes, or the weeds we pick from our garden and toss away, or the emotions that run through the system of our body.

Everything ends and is in constant flux. This is logical, like a river flowing, constantly changing form, so what we are doing is going with the flow of change and beginning to consciously change toward a more desirable result. Normally we are slaves to our brain. The brain sends electrical impulses, creating emotions, or feelings, which cause us to act accordingly.

This creates results in our lives. Sometimes just the energy we vibrate out is enough to attract a result with little or no action physically. When we begin to be mindful of what is going on, this gives us the freedom and power to change it. In this way we change our habits and our thoughts (thought energy), which changes the emotional energy, which in turn changes our actions and/or what we are attracting. Our thoughts lead to our emotions, which prompt us to act.

Thoughts are sending energy waves through your body. Feel the inner winds like tides in the ocean. Understand them. If you cannot figure out the energy or emotion, write about it, think it out, talk to someone you trust. Whatever the process is, we can learn to know the energy. We are not trying to destroy the energy, yet we are attempting to change it. So in essence, we must destroy the view we have about it. Like a fire that consumes a piece of wood, it may seem that the wood is being destroyed. But what is happening is that it is changing form, becoming smoke, which unites with other elements, ash and so on. We see it as destroying, and we can call it destroying or transforming, but whatever we call it, notice that this happens to all things.

The human body is constantly changing. We are not the same body physically that we were ten or twenty years ago: our skin cells are constantly shedding. New bone matter is being created and destroyed. Depending on what we put in our bodies, we are building new bodies on a constant basis.

How wonderful that we can consciously change, become the master of our brain instead of the servant. The brain is an amazing tool when used correctly. Yet, when we allow it to rule us, it uses fear and delusion in an ignorant attempt to protect us. Instead, let us be the master, and we will soon realize that the brain can be the perfect servant or coworker.

You are the boss, so now we will begin to take charge of our lives.

The Second Meditation
Using Meditation for Insight and Transformation

Know thyself. ~ Socrates

Now that we have a basic understanding of energy, we can begin to bring mindfulness into our practice to simply become aware of what is going on in our bodies. Awareness and understanding is the summit of change. If we don't understand something, it is not easily changed. The Buddha gave us a basic understanding that our happiness does not depend on manipulating the external world. He taught that it is much easier than that: we simply must see ourselves clearly. The meditation I am about to outline helps us to be aware of the emotions that arise within us. An emotion is the result of a thought, and that emotion leads us to act or react in such a way that our reality is created. Although it is nearly impossible to monitor all of our thoughts, it is much easier to monitor our emotions in particular situations. Emotions are like the loudest voice in a sports stadium. If you have ever been to a large sporting event, the voices of the tens of thousands of people just sound like an ocean, yet there is always that one person who yells the loudest. You can hear that one voice above all the rest. That is like emotional energy. We have tens of thousands of thoughts a day, yet the strong emotional energy we feel in any moment is like that one loud guy in the stadium. We can start there, with the loudest voice, the most prominent emotion we notice in the body.

I remember when I first started to do this meditation. I was having a hard time with someone I worked with. I used to work in television production, and we would work long hours and often have stressful days. One woman I worked with seemed to have the knack to be able to say exactly the right thing to me at exactly the right time to set me off. I am a pretty easy going guy, but she seemed to know how to push most people's buttons. I would feel anger arising within me and would often react, resulting in a fight or bicker that I would later regret. Or I would say nothing. I would just stuff the pain of anger down and go about my business. But later I would wonder why my back hurt so badly.

Remember the section on suppression?

On and on this went, and it was around this time that I began studying and practicing meditation in New York City. I remember learning this technique and applying it to this situation. I would sit in meditation in my bedroom in my Queens apartment and allow the situation of the woman to arise. I would literally replay it in my mind. I would feel the anger arising in me, and just notice it without engaging in it or pushing it away and suppressing it. I was in the habit of getting angry in this situation.

I remember another person I worked with who seemed to easily let it go, whereas I could not. There I was, all alone in my apartment, far from the woman I worked with: yet the same emotion was coursing through my body. It was at this juncture of the mediation that I used a bit of analytical thought, as I was taught. I realized that it is in fact my mind that is creating this emotion of anger, like a projector on a movie screen. In short I practiced allowing this anger to arise and simply move through me without grasping at it, following it, or suppressing it. I just allowed myself simply to be aware of it.

This was nearly impossible to practice when it happened at work, so I had to do it in my apartment in sitting meditation. My teacher called it my *laboratory*. When I went to work, sure enough the situations came up again, with her making comments or saying things that incited anger within me. I would allow the anger to pass through by going for a walk to the bathroom or sitting patiently at my computer, with my attention on my breath and just inwardly feeling the emotion.

Without realizing it, I was practicing stopping: I was not reacting to her words but was responding with mindfulness. The result was amazing. Over time she stopped directing those words or comments towards me, possibly because she received no reaction from me or because perhaps now she started to realize her actions toward me in the silence of her words. I am unsure of the exact reasons in her mind.

She would still, however, act in her usual manner towards others, because that was her habit. In my case, however, we ended up becoming good friends because outside of her habit in stressful situations to berate others she was, after all, a good person.

I started applying this to everything, not only people but situations also—in any situation that would incite an emotion. When the emotion would arise, I would start transforming it, with mindfulness, to an emotion that empowered me in my life. Soon I was transforming my reality at every turn.

If you have a recurring situation such as this one, it is also good sometimes to have a plan of what you might say or do when the situation arises. This way, when the situation does arise, you will not be caught off guard. You will have a skillful way of dealing with it, sometimes say-ing nothing says it all. Remember to be skillful in this plan: anger and arrogance are not skillful in the least.

This is not to say that we keep ourselves in harmful situations if they occur over and again. If someone is harming us, it is with mindfulness and clarity and the understanding that arises out of this practice that we will easily take ourselves out of harm's way.

It is when we are in the deluded mode of reactions—of guilt, anger, and so forth—that we actually keep ourselves in these situations. I did end up leaving my job. As I transformed my inner self, I was beginning to hold true to my heart, and my life had transformed in amazing ways.

The Laboratory Meditation

Sit in a comfortable place with the back straight, but relaxed. You can even do this lying down, but be careful not to fall asleep, which is why I recommend sitting. Take a moment to relax the mind and body. Per-haps do a few rounds of breathing, as described previously. When you find you are in a calm space, just allow the situation you wish to deal with to arise in your mind. Notice the emotional energy that is pro-jected into your body and notice where you feel it. Is it a specific spot in the body, perhaps a tingling or warm feeling throughout the entire body? Just be present with it, without grasping at it or pushing it away. This is not as easy as it sounds, because we are in the habit of running away from painful states of being. Yet I ask you just to allow it to be there, accept it. Stay with this for a little while, a few minutes at least, no matter how uncomfortable. Then begin to contemplate as follows: Where is this feeling? Begin to think the following: *I am sitting in med-itation. I am not actually in this situation. Yet, I feel the same as if I were.* Noticing that the mind is projecting this emotional energy onto your body like a projection on a screen, you can begin to breathe it away and allow it to pass through you. You may even want to name the delusion to accomplish this. It is as if we are watching a scary movie in a theatre. Fear arises, and we become scared. Movies are set up to create this false reality. Yet, if we look around, we see the screen, the projector, and we calm down, knowing we are in a theatre and there is no threat. Soon, though, we get back into the movie, and it grips us again. The same is true for the projections of mind.

Noticing this, just allow it to pass through you, and as you come to that peaceful place, just abide there, bathing in that space of peace, familiarizing your mind with it.

In this meditation you are getting to know the energies that cause you pain and suffering, and you are beginning to change the habitual patterns that keep you locked in these patterns. We can use this meditation in conjunction with *root writing*, where we have the insight or *aha* moment and hold it then dismantle it with the insight that our mind is creating this emotion and we are free to let this thought go.

Experiment with this and use it as it works for you. This is a process, so don't set the bar too high. Work off of your small success, and they will become your big successes with patience and persistence.

We need to develop compassion for ourselves, it is important not to be too hard on yourself. If you are practicing these techniques and see yourself falling back into the pattern, no worries, just keep at it. Be a warrior. It takes patience and a strong resolve to change patterns we have been following our entire lives, but we have the methods and the people to show us the way. We are never alone. We can tap into the energies of the masters or whoever or whatever that brings us inspiration. If one person can do it, so can you. We are all interconnected.

Let us review here what we have been practicing.

    1. Stopping: Learning to just stop and breathe. When we learn to stop what we are doing and calm our emotions, this is the first step where we begin to move away from reactive patterns that cause harm. We can also put our emotions on paper by using writing when emotions and anxieties are very strong, as opposed to getting caught in the reactive mind. This will teach us to be strong and solid like a tree. We can do this all day, while drinking tea, we can stop and be present, while driving, sitting on the beach, working, and so on. In this step we are simply learning not to blindly follow our reactions and get hijacked by our emotions.

2. Recognizing and Accepting: We accept the emotion that arises, calling it by its name. In this way we can then embrace what we usually push away and suppress or conversely engage in. In accepting painful emotions, we are not saying that it is okay that these emotions are harming us, as they often do. We are just accepting them and observing so we can begin to understand them. We can embrace the emotion, like a child who is crying. We can embrace our painful emotions like a mother holding a crying child. And only then can we begin to see why the child is crying.

As we name the delusion and accept it, instead of pushing it away and suppressing it, it begins to lose its hold over us already. We begin to decipher the weeds from the flowers. Then we can begin to plant the garden we wish to grow.

3. **Insight:** After we have calmed the delusion, we can begin to dismantle it. We can reflect on the causes and conditions of why this arises until we have some insight. Never engage in delusions while they are active, because they are manipulative and will convince you that they are right. You will only further engage in delusion. Simply accept an emotion without judgment. Again, writing helps us to allow the energy to flow through us, as opposed to holding onto it as we often do.

By looking deeply, we can reflect on the causes and conditions that have caused the emotion to arise. We can begin with the primary cause that set this habit off, but then look further into the other causes. As we trace it back, we may be surprised to find that what set us off initially may have little to do with the reactive emotion, which is very strong. We look deeply, either by thinking, writing, or talking out loud until the penny drops and we have that "aha" moment of realization. We can hold that realization in our minds to seal it in, and then we let it go.

4. **Resting:** In sitting meditation we allow ourselves to rest fully in that peaceful awareness. Allowing the body to be at peace and the mind to rest, we seal in the realizations and begin to heal

with the compassion of rest. So we just allow ourselves to rest, without worry, because resting is a prerequisite for healing. Sleep and lying down is only one way to rest. We can work without struggle, write without struggle, read joyfully, we can bring rest and joy into whatever we are doing. We need to train our minds and bodies to relax in this culture of action-dominated mind sets. There is no need to *do* anything, just be in the moment and enjoy what you are doing, without struggle.

Take time to rest. Have a day of rest. Go to the beach or do whatever helps you to strengthen the habit of relaxation. This will not only create the habit for rest in your life, but will also strengthen your nervous system. Rest activates the parasympathetic nervous system and strengthens the entire nervous system. And a strengthened nervous system means a healthy body and mind. When we practice resting without worry our bodies and minds heal themselves.

5. Replace: Now we can begin to replace the negative habits and emotions with empowering ones. Often this happens automatically. Many times when I work on something and have a realization, the empowering mind just arises out of wisdom. Yet, we can consciously do this as well. We can replace miserliness with generosity and so forth. When we are able to stop and accept and understand why we engage in these habits, we can now allow them to pass through us. When they do, we can replace them with empowering thought habits. The more we do this, the weaker the negative habit becomes. This can take time. So practice patience and persistence. With time you will create the new habit.

Stopping, calming, and resting are preconditions for healing. So practice them in all you do.

Meditation is self-healing. By calming, we tap into the restorative power of rest and inaction, which make our actions more enjoyable and more fruitful in all respects. Remember the balance of inaction and action. Both are needed in this process.

The Phases of Changing a Habit

When we wish to create a new habit, we must know that it takes practice, patience, and consistency. There are phases of learning a new habit, skill, or ability. I remember when I first learned to ride my bike. My mother would hold the back of the seat, and I would begin to peddle fast as she let go. I had to think about the peddling. My balance was wobbly, and stopping the bike was a whole new adventure. I remember I had to crash the bike the first time, because I was going so fast and I didn't yet have the habit (ability) yet to stop.

In time, riding a bike became second nature to me. I didn't have to think about it. I would practically live on my bike for most of my childhood. I could ride that bike with my eyes closed. I remember being able to stand on the seat as the bike was moving. All of our habits progress like this. At first we don't understand the new skill or habit, and often we don't even recognize the benefits it will have for us. Next, we attempt to learn the new skill, because we realize it could be of benefit to us in some way, often this is the toughest phase. I remember this phase when I learned to play the guitar, it seemed as though I would never get better. But I did.

The third phase is when we now know how to ride the bike or play the guitar, but it still takes a bit of concentrated effort to do so. This brings us to the final phase, where the skill or habit has become second nature to us: we hop on a bike without a thought, we strum the guitar with our eyes closed, not needing to think about it. In the world of psychology and education these are call the Four Stages of Competence and are called unconscious incompetence, conscious incompetence, conscious competence, and unconscious competence. Don't worry, I will explain this cluster of words more simply. Let's look at these four stages of competence, or phases of ability as I like to call them, in relation to changing our reactive habits of emotion that tend to control us and create undesirable results in our lives. As we begin to work with the methods outlined in this book, we will naturally move through these phases, so understanding them will give us the power to accept each phase, knowing we will make progress.

Phases of changing our habit energy:

Phase 1
In this phase our jealousy, anger, or other afflictive emotion arises, and we react without even recognizing that we are reacting. It just seems to be who we are and what we do—an almost unconscious action or reaction.

Phase 2
We now recognize that anger, jealousy, miserliness, or fear arises, but we still allow it to create our reactions. Even if we fight the urge to react, we just can't help ourselves. This is the toughest phase, and the one where most people give up, thinking they can never overcome this habit energy. Don't give up because no matter how strong the emotion is and no matter how many times we allow it to hijack our actions, this is a necessary step in the progression. You will never fail if you never give up. This is where we need to bring in patience and self-compassion, being gentle with ourselves and not beating ourselves up when we do act out of a deluded sense of mind.

Phase 3
In this phase delusion arises, we feel the energy of it in our body, but we don't allow the emotion to act itself out through us. We do not follow it, and conversely, we do not suppress it. We practice stopping and patient acceptance and allow it to pass through us without acting it out. Sometimes it takes days or hours to pass, but eventually it does pass. Perhaps you need to use writing to get it out, you may need to go for a long walk away from the person or situation that sparked it. Or you can use any of the numerous techniques we have been practicing so far. At this phase you begin to bring clear thinking into the oth-erwise clouded mind of delusion. Perhaps you realize that the person who said something to you making you angry has recently lost his or her job or is going through a tough time and is just irritable. You may realize that the remark really had nothing to do with you, or that the person just suffers on deeper levels. Their cockiness or arrogance is just a cover for the pain they feel. Whatever the situation, we begin to bring wisdom into it, remember that wisdom means to *see clearly*: a mind that gets stuck in a delusion of anger, jealousy, greed, and so

forth is the opposite of a clear mind. So in order to get to the clear mind of understanding, we practice stopping and allowing afflictive emotions to pass. Patience is key. This does not mean we become a passive doormat. Patience is a strength. It takes a warrior-like determination to walk away from a situation that makes us angry or to confront our greedy or jealous minds. It is easy to react with anger, but reaction is a weak state of being. We allow ourselves to be controlled by our delusions. On the other hand, the warrior is always in control, always stable and centered. When the storm of delusion arises, the warrior accepts that it is there, without the need to follow it. Such a demeanor is anchored in true strength, and every one of us has the potential for that warrior-like determination. Such a warrior is not the type that makes war on another. That's not valiant. The warrior who sets out to know himself or herself, in order to serve others, exhibits true valor.

Phase 4

In this phase the reaction energy doesn't even arise, and if it does, it is not as strong. in fact, often you forget that you had that energy arise in these situations. When the energy does arise, it is short lived, and you know how to let it pass through without letting it take control of you.

Keep these phases in mind as you work with your habits. The waves of energy that once manipulated and controlled your every action will become smaller and smaller as you engage in them less and less.

CHAPTER 10
INTERCONNECTION

All things are connected. Whatever befalls the earth befalls the sons of the earth. Man does not weave the web of life; he is merely a strand of it. Whatever he does to the web, he does to himself. ~ Chief Seattle

A mystical and wise monkey named Kavi in my novel *Shambhala* talks of how we are all a reflection of the Earth from which we came. Our bodies are composed of three quarters liquid and one quarter mass, like the Earth. Our veins and capillaries are like the rivers and streams. We have energy centers that run various systems of our bodies, just like the Earth. Like the Earth, our bodies can flush out toxins, but if they are too overwhelmed by toxins they will break down.

A great quote from Kavi is, "You are all things on Earth, and all things on Earth are you."

Let's think about this further for a moment, logically and scientifically. Your body that is sitting here now—your physical body inside and out—is just the result of the massive amount of food that you have eaten throughout your life. This food was grown in the Earth, fertilized by countless bugs and other beings that died and broke down to create nutrients in the soil, grown and cultivated by others, nourished by the sun and the rains, picked and harvested, processed, packaged, and transported, and then prepared for you by others. Therefore, your body is a result of the efforts of others. Or in the very least, the result of infinite conditions that came together to create what you call *your body*. Let's look at this a little deeper: your genetics were given to you by others; your language, even your name was given to you by others. All of our conditions are due to the causes and conditions of others.

So then, where is the Self?

Uh oh, the big question: here comes the airy fairy mystical stuff, right? Wrong. We can stay very practical here. The fact is that *self* cannot exist without others. Everything depends on everything else to exist. In fact, even the word *self* can't exist without other. In the most simplistic form, we can look at our Earth and how what we do to the Earth affects us. When we create genetically modified foods or spray toxins on the food we eat, we suffer cancers and famines for the simple fact that everything is interdependent and what we do to the Earth we do to ourselves.

We can see this in our everyday existence: choose to smile at someone and say a nice word and the ripple you create will be far different from one if you choose to frown and say something nasty to that person. A simple rule of thumb is to be kind and enjoy, or at least try to, because we are then creating this for all others, and in effect ourselves, because all we are is other. The wisdom of our interconnection makes us grateful for all of life on this Earth. There is a delicate flow of life. We breathe in oxygen created by the trees and plant life and expel carbon dioxide, which in turn feeds them.

So back to the big question: Where is the self. What brings us hardship and pain often is the view that we are separate, apart from others—independent. But as we just discussed, we are all a part of others. All we are is others. All we are is dependent on others.

Mother Teresa's observations of the world concluded, "The biggest disease today is not leprosy or tuberculosis, but rather the feeling of not belonging." She also noted that, "If we have no peace, it is because we have forgotten that we belong to each other." These profound statements by Mother Teresa illustrate the feelings of deep insecurity and disconnection we have with the world. We foster this unrealistic view that we are separate from all others and things in this world, when the truth is that all we are is due to the circumstances of others and in essence all we are is other.

While I was working on a documentary film in college about the rising problem of homelessness on Long Island, I had the good fortune to spend some time with a wonderful woman named Sister Elaine Bohrer. Sister Elaine started the Light House Mission on Long Island, whose mission is to feed the hungry and help the homeless. The closing line in the film is from an interview with her, and her simple yet powerful words stuck with me since that day: "We all need each other and that's what makes it work."

The fact is that we all are each other, and the wise ones have realized that by helping others we are helping ourselves. What I have found to be an effective way to overcome depression and insecure thoughts of separation is to volunteer to help others. This outward view and focus on others gives us back that sense of belonging and worth. Lao Tzu, the great master of the Tao, said, "Serve the needs of others, and your own needs will be fulfilled." When we become the source of something, whether it's love, abundance, belonging, or anything, we are creating it in our lives as well, because there is no separation between me and another. When we become the source of what we want and create it for others, we naturally create it for ourselves.

Perceptions: How the Mind Separates the Whole

I came to realize clearly that mind is no other than mountains and rivers and the great wide earth, the sun and the moon and the stars. ~ Dogen

Our entire world is viewed through the lens of our perceptions. How we view ourselves, others, and objects. Our entire world is created by the thoughts we project outward from the beliefs and conditions we have built since childhood. We experience things as being independent and outside of the mind, but our experience of life is just a projection of the mind. In our power to perceive is our power to create the experience. This is our intimate connection with all that is. Because everything exists only in the way I perceive it to, I am deeply and intimately connected to all things in this way.

I am not saying that things do not conventionally exist. Things exist: I sit in a chair right now as I write on my computer. I do not deny that my body is here, fingers tapping away on the keys. Brian exists, yet I don't exist the way others perceive me to exist. Even I view myself through the lens of my own perceptions, so I only exist to myself the way I perceive myself. And I exist to you only the way you perceive me as well. We often see someone or something through the lens of our perceptions and have a fixed view of it as static and unchanging, when the reality is that everything is constantly changing, in constant flux. For example, if I had a piece of chocolate cake and presented it to two people, one may say, "Yum I love chocolate cake!" The other may have had a negative experience with cake in the past and think, "Yuk I can't stand chocolate cake." This cake now exists as two different things, one that is a source of pleasure and goodness and the other as a source of aversion and disgust, when in reality it is just a piece of cake that is dependent on an infinite amount of circumstances to exist. Perhaps I left the sugar out of the cake, when the chocolate cake lover takes a bite, he or she may grimace and think, "Yuk I don't like that chocolate cake."

This is a simplistic example of what we are doing all the time to things and people, including ourselves. We may think, *He is an angry person, she is a spiritual person*, and so on. Both things and people are constantly changing; our bodies and minds are in a state of constant flux and in fact are conditions that depend on many factors to exist.

All masters have realized that by changing our minds, our perceptions, we change our lives and the world around us. Einstein said, "The most important decision we make is whether we believe we live in a friendly or hostile universe." The decision is ours, and in fact many believe that the only real choices we have are in how we experience the perfection all around us. We have the choice to experience the moment, and it starts with our thoughts, which create the emotion, and thus how we experience life.

Ralph Waldo Emerson once said, "Great men are they who see that spiritual is stronger than any material force—that thoughts rule the world." We have been investigating how our beliefs and views create our thoughts, which create emotions that lead us to action, or inaction, which physically create our worlds. The simple act of shifting our perceptions can be very powerful in our lives.

There was a woman known as Peace Pilgrim who walked the Earth bringing her message of peace to all who would listen. She once said, "If you knew how powerful your thoughts were, you would never think a negative thought." Our minds are very powerful tools and players in creating our reality, so wouldn't it be wise to be able to go in and shift our perceptions?

I recently heard a person talking about a celebrity, saying how she didn't like him because he was a jerk and a pig. I asked her if she knew him. She replied that she didn't but had heard a story of him doing something or acting in some way one day. I asked her if she ever had a bad day or a time she regretted saying or doing something. Of course she had, don't we all? I then proposed that perhaps this man is not as bad as she perceived. Perhaps he was having a bad day. And in his case, the bad day or act gets publicized worldwide.

I do not know this man, and wasn't defending him, but was pointing out the fact that we fix people into labels. We do this with ourselves all the time: we may have screwed something up or perhaps we were picked last for the baseball games in gym class, and now we have this perception that we are a bad baseball player. *I must be terrible*, we think, *I screwed up in the last game, I am always picked last*. Even if we are a mediocre player we have the power to change if we wish. Yet we will never change if we keep the fixed perception of being a bad baseball player.

Think of a perception you hold about yourself and analyze why you see yourself as such. If it is negative and you wish to change it, investigate all the causes and conditions that led to that belief and perception. Perhaps it started when you were told something as a child.

So who do you think you are? Make a list of ten things you perceive yourself to be. Try doing five positive and five negative. Now look at the five negative things and investigate why you perceive yourself to be this. What can you do to change that perception of yourself? Do you perceive yourself to be lazy? Why? What actions can you take to change this? Remember it starts with the view, the perception, then the action. If we are lazy, chances are we have a view of ourselves as being such, and so we live up to that view. Yet, once we change our inner world of perceptions, our outer world changes as well.

Do you wish to be a slave to the perceptions of others, or the perceptions of yourself? You can never control how others perceive you, but you can control how you perceive yourself. Do not worry or fret how others see you. If I give a talk to 2,000 people, there will be 2,000 different perceptions of who I am. But the only one that really matters is the perception I have about myself. When we change our perceptions, we change the way we look at ourselves and thus change ourselves. When we change our perceptions of the world and other people, we do the same. It is your choice.

We can practice observing our preconceived notions of others as well. We may see a homeless man, and all these preconceived notions may come flooding in: perhaps that man is an enlightened being or perhaps not, but we will never really know if we allow the prison of preconceived notions to keep our minds narrow. Maybe we see a holy man and think he or she is all knowing and good. He may well be, but may not be as well. The movie *Kumare* comes to mind, in which a man pretends to be a guru: he dresses like one, grows his hair long, and wears a beard. He plays off of the perceptions of what others believe a guru should look like and be, when in fact he is just a hip, thirty-three-year-old filmmaker from New Jersey pretending to be an Indian guru, or at least that's the perception he projects.

The words from the wise Baba in *Shambhala* come echoing in, "Sometimes what we see isn't necessarily what is there." This is not to say there aren't dynamic, wonderful people in the world, or despicable ones who cause much harm, but when we allow the automatic response of preconceived notions to mold the man, we aren't really being very open minded to the possibilities.

When we realize that everything is only a perception of the mind—it exists, but it doesn't exist the way we perceive it to exist—then we realize that we have a beautiful and intimate connection with everything and the ability to change it simply by changing our mind, which is perceiving it. You may say, "I don't care how much I change my mind, this person will always be rude and difficult." To a mind that perceives the other to be difficult and sees only a shallow flaw in another, then yes, but wisdom will reveal a person who suffers, a person who may be misunderstood, and perhaps then we can change our view from one of annoyance and avoidance to one of understanding and compassion toward another. This is one example of many.

Let us start with ourselves and the things we see in our world. Again I ask you, "Who do you *think* you are?" Because as Henry Ford said, "Whether you think you can, or you think you can't—you're right."

A Constant in the World of Consistent Change

There is a divine dance going on in the universe, and we are all part of the whole, each one of us a strand in the proverbial quilt of life. Things are constantly changing and moving, the constant ebbs and flows of life, birth and death, on many levels: the sun rises and moves across the sky, then sinks, giving rise to the moon.

We just learned how our perceptions create our realities, but changing perceptions is more easily said or read than done. To reiterate, things exist, *I* am here writing this. Brian is sitting here, but everyone in this café where I write this is perceiving Brian differently. Even I perceive myself as different from all of them. The Brian they perceive to exist exists only because of the mind that perceives it to. You think, "Brian," and then fix me as some unchanging thing, but Brian is just a result of others, constantly changing like a flowing river.

We tend to fix others and even ourselves in this static position, unchanging, but the truth is that everything is flowing and changing. Every bite of food or bit of information we ingest changes us, and we change it as well. Every person we come into contact with, our various environments, all change us and we change them as well.

This is powerful when we begin to understand this because when we change our perceptions, we change the world around us. Gandhi said, "Our greatness lies not so much in being able to remake the world as in being able to remake ourselves." Again, things exist even though at times I hear people talk of how everything is an illusion. Well, this is partially true: the illusion lies in the perception that things inherently exist. Yet they don't exist the way our minds judge them to exist, based on our views of the past. That's the illusion or delusion often: they simply just exist as parts of the whole.

As we learned earlier, because of these views we have from our past we often relate to a limited, fixed self. We even say in our language, "I am angry or I am sick." Some other languages are set up a little better where they say, "I have anger," or "I have sickness", or "I have anger arising." These expressions suggest more accurately what is really happening. The Hopi language is even more accurate: there are no nouns. In Hopi, for instance, there are no clouds, but "clouding"; no stream, but "streaming"; no anger, but "angering." This is similar to the Sanskrit expression for "ego," *ahamkara*, which means "I (*aham*) making (*kara*), " one's ongoing activity of sensing oneself as separate from all else. In each case nouns are expressed as verbs, as ongoing actions that are constantly changing and thus capable of evolution.

On the other hand, when we fix the passing emotion, allowing it to limit who we are, we limit ourselves and fix ourselves as being that. Yet, logic and science prove that everything is changing in every moment. This is truth. I couldn't finish this sentence if it weren't: we'd all sort of be frozen here in time. Fundamentally if there were no change, nothing could happen.

Much change we perceive as good. I love to watch the waves change shape and crash on the shore, technology changes at a rapid rate and gives us many amazing advancements in science. We also perceive much change as not so good. Our bodies age and become old and break down, our relationships change, and we often lose those that we love. Eventually there's death: everything we hold will be gone sooner than we think.

Change can be stressful whether we view it as good or bad. When we really look, each moment disappears the instant it arises. This can be stressful, especially to us human animals, who like habitual routine. Time goes by so quickly: as soon as something pleasant passes by the mind, it's gone before we realize it. Anything that changes is not a reliable source for lasting contentment or fulfillment then, is it? How could it be, it's fleeting. So where can we find lasting contentment? Seemingly nowhere in this world, which can be tiresome and daunting because as soon as we seem to find contentment or happiness, it changes, and so what we grasp at slips through our fingers as quickly as it came.

All the masters have taught that underlying all that changes there is something that stays the same—beginningless and endless. This is the peaceful stillness that pervades us all. Lao Tzu reminded us that "to know harmony is to know the changeless; to know the changeless is to have insight." This is what some have called God, the Source, ultimate reality, the Tao, Brahman, Now, the void and so on. The fact is that this is not something we can intellectualize. It can only be experienced, and meditation helps us to familiarize with this, so we can begin to live this in even the most chaotic of situations.

We don't have to realize enlightenment in order to experience this; we can begin to realize it all around us every moment. The world and your body changes every second, but you can always bring your awareness to the stillness, the peace in each moment. Using the breath is a good way to do this. We can bring our awareness to the present moment, back to our breath whenever we feel we begin to slip away into chaotic thought or situations. We can do breath meditation to train the mind to be present and less distracted by chattering thoughts. In any moment, we can use that constant of stillness to realize our limitless potential.

We were just talking about perceptions: our perceptions lead us to react in certain ways. For example someone says something to us and our habit is to react with anger. We can practice stopping, and like all things the anger (or what the Hopi would call the "angering") will pass (fade away like a "clouding"). Perhaps we go for a walk or use writing to allow it to flow through us, and in that space of stillness we can then create what we want skillfully in the situation. We can now begin to use wisdom (seeing clearly) as opposed to delusion to create our reality. We now begin to become conscious creators as opposed to reactive animals. Again, mindfulness is the key, and meditation helps to cultivate mindfulness.

Lao Tzu said, "If you realize that all things change, there is nothing you will try to hold onto." He also reminded us that, "contentment alone is enough. Indeed, the bliss of eternity can be found in your contentment."

Everything is temporary. You can remind yourself of this when you are going through a hard time or when anger or jealousy or any other painful emotion arises. Know that it will arise and pass away, like all things do. There is no reason to grasp at it or engage in it, simply accept it and realize that it too will pass away. The proof that our nature is peace and joy is that when the delusions of anger and so forth pass by, we are left with peace.

Inertia is when you throw a ball up in the air, it pauses before it comes back down. That pause—the space between breaths, the space between thoughts—is the silence where creation takes place. Like a beautiful composition of music, it's the space between the notes that creates the music. We can all learn to tap into this by simply learning to stop and breathe.

How we can use this space to create?

Here are some points on this powerful creation process:

1. When a situation arises causing a negative, reactive emotion, we practice stopping. (We can write or go for a walk, but do not engage the afflictive emotion or suppress it.)

2. Once the emotion moves away and we can come into that peaceful stillness, we can begin to insert what we wish to create. (We can substitute generosity for miserliness, compassion in place of hatred or confidence and trust in place of jealousy.) In this way we are now creating our reality consciously as opposed to having it created unconsciously, led by our delusions. We can now skillfully think, *What do I wish the outcome to be?* We can become conscious creators now within that space.

3. Watch our reality begin to reshape: be patient and persistent and you will see amazing results.

In Part 2 of this book we will delve more deeply into manifesting in this way.

Chapter 11
Proper Relaxation

To be calm is the highest achievement of the self. ~ Zen Proverb

A tired body and mind are a breeding ground for delusion. Think of when you are tired: you become cranky, perhaps snap at people, irritate easily. Maybe you're one to get whiney. Everyone reacts differently to the stress of exhaustion, but any current issue in our lives tends to become magnified and often very oppressive when we are tired. Life just isn't as enjoyable as it is with a rested body and mind. In our culture, we find it difficult to be restful. We may lie on the couch all day, yet the mind is busy and full of work. We can sit all day at work and be exhausted by the mental pressures it places on us. There is a balance and harmony that needs to be met in life if we wish to operate at optimal performance. There must be a balance between action and inaction in both mind and body; inaction is an important element for action. The inaction makes for not only more fruitful actions but also gives us the ability to enjoy the actions more. Most successful people know the benefits of rest and recreation in the formula for success, true success, which is not only monetary. Some people gain massive success monetarily, yet are burnt out, have declining relationships and a general lack of joy and fulfillment in their lives. That does not sound like true success to me. We need balance, and proper relaxation is a key element that can bring it all together.

In yoga we learn *savasana*, which is Sanskrit for "corpse pose." This is the asana where we lie on the floor and consciously relax the body between poses and at the end of our practice. Although this is the pose many people like because we are simply lying down, it is said to be the hardest pose to master. The reason being is that the goal is to be like a corpse, to detach from the mind and body so the mind and body can heal and rest. This pose also trains us to practice relaxing all day. We have such trouble relaxing that even when we are on vacation we often don't know how to relax. We need to learn to get into that space of relaxation, that space of peace and rest. This is where some of the best ideas come from in business, writing, art, or whatever it is you may be doing in life.

Sounds easy enough, right? Well many people are thinking as they read this, *I have no time to rest*. Perhaps the demands of your life don't permit time to just stop and relax often. Well, the good news is that we can practice relaxing all day. As I write this, I can write with joy and relaxation. I don't need to be tense. Being tense is a habit, a fight-or-flight reactionary mind. Yet, we can change this destructive habit that only serves to bring stress to our lives.

Often I practice relaxing every time I sit down, be it on the subway, at a desk, or anyplace: I take five or ten seconds to bring my attention to my body and consciously relax it. I often find my shoulders are tense or jaw is clenched, and I didn't even notice this.

We can go all day with shoulders or back tight and jaw clenched.

Try this right now for five seconds, go on I'll wait...

Congratulations you just did a five-second meditation.

Did you notice any unnecessary tension in the face, brain, forehead, or shoulders? The more we bring awareness to this destructive habit, the more we relax and soon we will develop a new habit for relaxation. It is often good to have a suggestion, something that reminds us to relax. For example whenever I am in New York City and I get onto a subway and sit, I consciously relax my mind and body for a minute, and joy comes flooding in as a result. We must learn to be flexible and relaxed because a rigid and tense mind and body is one that breaks easily. It is a weakness, as opposed to a flexible mind and body, which bends in the wind like a piece of bamboo, strong and joyful.

Most religions and spiritual practices observe a day of rest, yet in our modern world these days of rest are not honored as they once were. I would advise a day of rest if possible: the benefits will be immense. You will find that there will be a vast difference in a day: one day you feel tired and defeated by the world, but when we take a day to rest, we become strong and ready to take on anything. The irony of working ourselves sick is that when one rests in between or takes a day of rest they are more likely to be successful in all areas of their lives and more effective at the tasks at hand, but we often ignorantly think we need to work, work, work—with no rest. There are countless success stories of people having their most lucrative ideas within a mandatory rest they have incorporated into their lives. One person in particular had told his family of his day of rest and would lock his door to the basement and was not allowed to be disturbed. He would rest his mind, watch a little TV, allow himself to be still, and as a result, he said most of his successes were bred from this time alone.

 Like a beautiful composition of music, it's the space between the notes as well as the notes that makes the music, or else it would just be one long sound, not very graceful. Our lives are often an ungraceful, long sound with no breaks. As we read earlier, even when we are sick, we have trouble resting. We worry, thinking, *Should I call the doctor? Oh, I can't believe I am sick!* And so on and on we disturb our rest with thoughts like this, even getting angry at the fact that we are sick. When an animal gets sick it retreats into a safe place and does nothing but rest. The animal doesn't take drugs to numb the pain and push through it. The animal doesn't worry about it much. The animal simply rests, and consequently will heal much faster than us. The body and mind have an amazing ability to heal themselves, all we need do is relax and keep a peaceful mind. The grand design of all animals, including humans, comes with a built-in need to sleep. Nature shows us simply, yet we often are deprived of proper sleep or have such a habit for a busy mind and body that even in sleep we do not rest properly.

I have found that we are so habitually conditioned to *do* that even when we do take a day of intended rest, the mind wants to do: it wants to search the web, it incessantly wanders to what we *should do*. Recognize that this is a habit. Some good practices I have used during a day of rest is to take a hot bath, perhaps with some Epsom salts. I sometimes take some valerian root (an herbal supplement) or drink some chamomile tea to help retrain this incessant habit energy that finds difficulty in resting. Sometimes I just stay in bed and try to keep a peaceful mind. I eat good food and drink plenty of water. These provide a good meditation that heals the mind and body, and the benefits the next day are immense.

Create your daily hypnotic suggestion now for rest. You can use anything such as the following: "Every time I wash my hands, I take ten seconds to bring awareness to my body and mind and relax any tension." The suggestion could be that anytime you see water or anytime you sit down, maybe every time you sit down at your desk at work, you bring awareness to the body and relax. We can even do this while driving. Often we tense up without noticing when driving, yet we can relax the body and mind. Often, if I just internally say, "Relax my brain," a couple of times, it sends a signal to my entire body to relieve unnecessary tension. You can use a sticky note maybe on your bathroom mirror or at your desk at work that says, "Relax." If you do use the sticky note, I would suggest moving it every couple of weeks, because as with everything in our lives we no longer see it after a short while.

Let's now briefly look at the benefits and science of being more restful. Often you will see a statue of an enlightened being such as the Buddha, made of pure gold. The gold represents a state of complete rest, zero stress. Zero stress means impenetrable to disease. Stress is the largest culprit in creating sickness of mind and body, and relaxation can combat this. The Buddha said, "My dharma is the practice of non-practice."

The autonomic nervous system (ANS), which regulates the functions of our internal organs, includes the sympathetic and parasympathetic nervous systems. The sympathetic nervous system (SNS) is the one that flares up in the fight-or-flight response when we feel threatened or excited, when we are chasing opportunities, or in emergencies and things of this nature. The parasympathetic nervous system (PNS) allows us to rest and digest. There is a healthy balance of the two in the body, yet in our culture we are more and more dominated by the SNS, and as a result have more stress than we should have. Again this is due to our habits: we are being trained and conditioned by our world to go-go-go, and often don't even know how to relax if we wanted to. This wreaks havoc on our immune systems and degenerates our brains and bodies: the chemicals that are released in fight-or-flight responses and stress-induced states can be very destructive if not regulated by the PNS. In fight-or-flight responses, the hormonal system shuts down to conserve energy for the fight. We need not think about sex while fighting or when running from a tiger: our digestion shuts down as well.

Again, we do not have to go to the bathroom in situations of emergency or fight or flight: this is why in extreme cases many go to the bathroom in their pants. When extremely scared, the digestion completely shuts down, and all comes out. In this state, blood is rushed to the legs for running, and in some cases this is helpful, as when evading a hungry tiger. But in our modern world, we turn on this system, and it never shuts off, leaving us with a huge rise in sexual dysfunction, digestion issues, and a myriad of other destructive immunity and mental health issues. Learning to stimulate the parasympathetic nervous system will bring calmness and joy to your life. You will become stronger in mind and body and overall healthier and more functional as a human being.

Throughout this book we have been exploring techniques to calm the mind and body and tap into the PNS. Learn what fits into your life, create a suggestion and a habit for rest. Simply taking a couple of deep diaphragmatic breaths can stimulate the PNS and counteract the SNS. We must learn to be the masters of our brains or else they will keep us stuck in a primordial fight-or-flight state, which is not joyful or beneficial to anyone.

The warrior is calm and peaceful and thus strong in body and mind.

A System of Calming the Body to Calm the Mind

There are many stages in mental development, but as soon as we are able to maintain the mind in a calm state, at that very moment there is joy and peace. This is reflected in the body becoming relaxed, and then the mind becomes more relaxed. As the mind calms down, the hidden enlightened qualities emerge more and more. ~ Venerable Khenpo Rinpoche

In the physical art of yoga, known as Hatha Yoga, we engage in *asanas* (Sanskrit for "poses"). There are various reasons for different asanas, but the main reason yogis do the physical practice of yoga is so they can sit for long periods of time in meditation. This is the goal of yoga. In yoga the meditation aspect is called Raja Yoga, the Royal Path. The goal is to achieve *God union*, to reunite with the natural peace and clarity that they call God. Some call this the source, heaven, the universe, and so on. Again, this is the all-pervasive peace, the truth of who we are, whatever you wish to label it, do so in that it resonates with you on the level of truth.

In yoga you are training the mind by first training its counterpart, the body. When the body is tight and inflexible, the mind is tight and inflexible, and vice versa. The body and mind are connected, and the breath is the intermediary, the bridge between mind and body.

Yoga nidra is a wonderful practice in yoga where you lie on the floor and are guided to complete relaxation of mind and body where you can easily come into that space of meditation. It's a sort of hypnosis. After all, hypnosis is simply a method to get you into a subconscious meditative space, where you are open to suggestion and can access the deeper levels of habit in the unconscious. *Yoga nidra* means "yoga sleep," but is sort of a misnomer, because you are not really sleeping. In fact, you are being guided into that space between waking and dreaming, the meditative space of healing where change can occur at deeper levels. In meditation, we are doing self-hypnosis at times, and this is wonderful because this is where we can access the deeper energies and begin to change them at the level of the subconscious mind.

What we are doing in this meditation is first relaxing the body, part by part. We start with the feet and move all the way up to the top of the head. We then move onto the internal organs, ending with the brain. And as we move through, we go deeper and deeper into meditation. This is a great method to guide you deep into meditation. Sometimes when you sit in meditation your mind and body are agitated. Combining this with some of the breathing ratios we have learned will help you to gain that middle ground of calm.

We are usually either in an agitated state of mind or a dull state of mind, so the breathing ratios are a wonderful way to balance this and get us to that steady state of mind. Likewise this method for calming the body will be helpful as well. Often we don't even have to go through the entire body: a simple few seconds of scanning the body and seeing what is tight, then relaxing it, can help guide us into a deeper sense of well-being and thus help us in our meditations. This is also a great method to use for those with insomnia or trouble sleeping.

A Method for Insomnia

By systematically relaxing your body from toes to brain, you more easily slip into a deep sleep. I recommend doing the yoga nidra body relaxation technique then the breath ratio of 4:2:7. For me, I often don't get to even four or five rounds before I am fast asleep. Often with not being able to sleep, the fear of not being able to sleep is arising and we push it away as we think, *I need to get to sleep and be up early tomorrow.* This makes the emotional energy of fear more prevalent, and the option for sleep further away. We ignorantly think that by pushing the fear away we will sleep faster, yet that is why we can't fall asleep: that feeling in our solar plexus or wherever it may be. The accepting and naming works well for this, as you lie there, accept the fear, the feelings that arise with this energy, and use what we have been practicing. It works very well here. Use all three of these methods to help you with this if need be. Make it your own and see what works best for you.

A Basic Explanation of Yoga Nidra

You can begin at the toes and feet if you like, simply saying internally, "Relax the toes and feet, my toes and feet are relaxing, my toes and feet are relaxed." Move your way all the way up to the top of the head, systematically relaxing the entire body. You can then move onto the internal organs if you wish in the same way, "Relaxing the stomach, my stomach is relaxing, my stomach is completely relaxed." Again, move through the organs until you get to the brain, and at this point, after you relax the brain, you will be in a deep state of relaxation. Try to bring your awareness to the area of focus and feel it relaxing as you send the message from your brain to that area by internally telling it to relax.

CHAPTER 12
OPPORTUNITY IN EVERYTHING, THE GLASS HALF FULL ATTITUDE

I once heard the story that someone had asked a Geshe, which is a high level Buddhist monk, "Hey Geshela, how are you doing?" He answered with a smile, "I am doing wonderful, I have so many problems." He wasn't joking, he actually lives his life with this truth, that all of his seeming problems are opportunities to learn and grow and eventually develop empathy and help others. This is true in all aspects of life, and if you look at some of the most successful people in business, sports, or any arena, you would find a similar outlook.

There are no problems, only opportunities. What makes something a problem verses an opportunity is the mind that perceives it. Many people see everything as a problem in their lives; they are in the habit of seeing only problems and little or no opportunity, and so what follows are series of problems, because we are what we think about. Conversely, those who view a seeming problem as an opportunity are presented with only opportunities, and they grow and become wise accordingly. Sometimes at points in our lives this task is daunting: everything seems to be going wrong.

I can recall several times in my life when the world seemed to be closing in on me. In hindsight these were the times I learned and grew the most and were the times that set me on my path ever stronger. As the old saying goes, "A smooth sea never made a skilled sailor."

The point is that it is wise to adapt this mind set and habit of seeing everything as an opportunity to learn and grow. It not only empowers you to greater success in all you do, but also empowers you to help others if you choose to do so. The mind set of the problem seer is one of inept insecurity. It takes courage to see opportunity, and when you begin to shift your mind from one of "Poor me and all my problems" to "This is an opportunity to learn, bring it on!" your world begins to change. Less and less *problems* arise, and more and more opportunities are presented to create more abundance, love, and joy in your life, enabling you to give that back to the world.

What would you choose to give the world, problems or opportunities? All it takes is a shift in perception.

Retraining the Mind for Success
Why our minds are set up for negativity
and how it affects our relationships

If you knew how powerful your thoughts are, you would never think a negative thought. ~ Peace Pilgrim

Why does it seem as if it takes more effort to cultivate positive mental states and habits then it does to cultivate negative ones? It seems as though negative habits and thoughts are effortless, whereas positive ones take effort and conscious awareness. This is because it does take more effort. Did you ever notice how our lovers, family members, or friends can do a thousand positive things, a thousand great acts toward us, but the one negative thing they do we harp on it as if that one negative thing negates the thousand. As soon as they do something we disapprove of we say, "How do I get them out of my life? That's it! This relationship is over!"

The reason this happens is because the brain is primordially set up to absorb negative thinking and experiences. In fact, it believes that it is crucial to our survival to do so. Way back when we were cavemen and women and we were walking through the woods, we needed to remember the time that tiger lunged from the bushes and gashed our arm before we narrowly escaped with our lives, more than we needed to remember how beautiful that flower was that we passed. The brain's survival instinct shields positive experiences so we can foster the negative in order to survive in the jungles that are our lives. You do live in the jungle don't you? Well not most of us, in fact this primordial function of the brain is quite outdated, and in our modern world can be very destructive to not only ourselves but those around us as well. The brain is designed to protect the separate self, protection of the individual is key here in the primordial fight-or-flight system. The brain is an amazing organ when used properly. Yet, we must learn to become the masters of our brains lest we allow them to rule us with fears and anxieties and an outdated program that serves only to cause more pain in our lives.

In primordial times, the constant anxiety that welled up when we entered the woods would serve as a warning system for us to stay on guard. Yet, in our modern world we can be mindful of what we are doing and where we are. We don't have to live in constant fear like wild animals. We don't need incessant anxiety and worry to protect us. If we put our hands on a hot stove, and it burns us, we have enough intelligence not to do it again: we don't need a constant anxiety about it and for it to dominate our brains unconsciously with fear—yet this is what happens. This is a simplistic example of what is going on all the time.

Fear has its place in our lives: we look both ways before we cross the street. But if that fear of getting hit by a car keeps us pinned to our bedroom walls and we never go out as a result, this can be unhealthy. We often lie in our beds completely safe from any harm, yet the brain keeps us locked in anxiety about something that might happen but isn't happening now, and usually it's something that never does happen. This ceaseless worry does not serve to help us in the situation at hand. In fact anxiety and worry lower our immune function and weaken muscle tissue, making us weaker and less capable of handling situations. Yet, the brain ignorantly believes it is protecting us by incessantly milling this in our minds.

Fear and negativity are just fantastic stories our minds create to try to protect us. Yet, the reality is that we are fine in this moment. As we sit here and read this, there is no danger, yet often, and perhaps right now, we may have fears and anxieties that take us from this present reality of perfection and peace. There is danger sometimes, but when we are mindful of each moment, we can easily divert danger as it comes, we don't need to obsess over it.

The ancient Samurai knew this. They were the greatest warriors on the battlefield. In the midst of chaos, anger, and fear all around them on the battlefield, they were centered and clear, and thus the greatest warriors on the field. They trained their minds to do just that, and meditation was a staple for the Samurai as a means of training the mind. Ironically, the worry and fears and anxieties take us from the present moment, actually making us more prone to danger. A clear mind in the present moment is a strong mind and body ready to combat anything if need be.

We can learn to train our minds in positive thinking, the average human brain has anywhere from 12,000 to 60,000 thoughts per day, and of these thoughts about eighty percent are negative.

Again, we see this in our relationships: our mate can do a thousand positive things, but the one negative thing he or she does, we harp on it and brood over it as if that one negative thing negates the thousand positive. We suddenly search for ways to rid that person from our lives. This is a primordial fight-or-flight reaction, so recognize this when it comes up.

In traditional yoga, we learn positive thinking. We learn to cultivate positive minds. Observe your thoughts, observe your relationships, and see what your thoughts are about those relationships. Many times when we first get into relationships, we are blinded by the massive surge of serotonin that courses through the brain. Our partner can do no wrong. This is called the *honeymoon phase*. Soon things settle down and we start to notice things that annoy us, and often we don't just notice them, but we brood over them. Soon we are looking at others, thinking how wonderful it would be to have a relationship with them. And so we leave our mates for another, and everything is great. They smell perfect. They say the right things. "Our soul mates!" we exclaim! But soon it happens again. After the honeymoon phase wares off, our primordial mind begins to shift to its eighty-percent negativity and starts creating all types of fantasies and stories of what's wrong with the other person and how maybe, just maybe there is someone better who won't have such negative aspects.

Well, I am here to say: turn the camera on yourself and observe those thoughts of the other. Try to shift to the twenty percent of positive thoughts, because what we focus on expands. And if we focus on the twenty percent of positive thoughts we have, we will begin to create a habit for positive thoughts and will foster the positive aspects in the ones who are close to us. This is not to say that some relationships just don't work out for whatever reason. Yet, applying this method to all of our relationships will do wonders for our brains and create a more positive outlook and attitude. People will start to take notice, because you will be calmer, friendlier, and more joyful.

Make a list of twenty positive qualities of your lover, close friend, family member, or coworker—and when you find the mind slipping to the negative harping of the primordial brain, pull out the list. We can do this with ourselves as well. Often we get down on ourselves, sometimes treating ourselves worse than we would any other. As we have learned, we can stop and recognize these negative mind patterns, and in any moment shift to a more positive thought. We can pull out our sheets of our twenty good qualities and focus the mind on those. Remember we are what we think about, and our world is also a result of those thoughts. So we might as well think positive thoughts.

It is not easy to just stop worrying or being angry and so forth. It takes insight and training the mind in new thought patterns. Meditation is paramount in helping us retrain the habits of mind we currently have. In the basic forms of meditation, we become more mindful and settle the fight-or-flight monkey mind that dominates us most of the day. A simple breath meditation just five minutes a day can have profound effects on your health, both physically and mentally, and could be the start of new, empowering habits of mind.

In any moment we can shift the focus on the good qualities about our self as well. We can choose to identify with the good, positive qualities of our self and others. This just needs to become a habit. So when you catch yourself focusing on the negative qualities, shift your focus. If you catch yourself, you will find that this is not that hard to do. So, like all things, we begin with recognizing that we are even doing it.

The Power of Gratitude

When you arise in the morning, think of what a precious privilege it is to be alive - to breathe, to think, to enjoy, to love. ~ Marcus Aurelius

Gratitude may be one of the most powerful creation tools in existence. It is so easy to get caught in the mundane stir of our hectic lives. And as we have learned, our brains are set up to absorb negative experiences and harp on the negative in our lives in an ignorant attempt to protect us. This primordial faculty of the brain makes it harder for us to appreciate what we have in life. Think of when you were going through a tough time and someone pointed out the good things in your life: you may have shrugged it off as not as important as the negative experience you were dealing with, or perhaps you just passively recognized it and then brought your full attention back to the negative experience. This is what most of us do in our daily lives. We have so much to be grateful for in our lives. And the fact is that by focusing on the positive in our lives we will attract more positive into our lives. Our entire world is a result of our thoughts, what we choose to focus on: so when we are grateful we open the gates for more opportunities to be grateful again. The great 13th-century German philosopher, mystic, and theologian Meister Eckhart told us, "If the only prayer you ever say in your entire life is thank you, it will be enough."

Gratitude is the open door to abundance. When we learn to appreciate the things we do have in our lives, we are inviting more of that into our lives. Conversely, the same is true for when we harp on the negative: we invite more negative into our lives. Put simply, we are meditating all the time. When we become angry, for example, we are masters of single-pointed meditation: nothing can take our minds from the experience or person who angered us. And thus, that meditation enforces the habit for anger and creates more opportunities for anger to arise in our lives. The same is true for all negativity in our lives. By allowing the power of gratitude to be a daily part of our lives we begin to shift our attention and change our lives dramatically.

There are many ways to cultivate the habit of gratitude and appreciation in our lives, a gratitude journal is a great way to do this. I found this a great way to shift my focus to one of gratitude. Every night before I went to bed I would write five things I was grateful for and just be with them for a moment. Sometimes I will just lie there before drifting off to sleep and think about what I am grateful for in my life. You will feel the higher vibrations of joy and gratitude well up within you when you practice this. We can do this all day long, training the mind to shift perspective from the negative *poor-me* mind that closes the door to the abundance we seek, to the grateful mind that opens the gate wide for positive opportunity to flow in.

A great habit to acquire is every morning just as you wake up tell yourself, "I love my life!" This invites the energy of gratitude, love, and joy into your day. Will you have bad days? Of course you will. Will you sometimes say this and it will seemed forced? Yes, it will. But the key is on those days to really bring to mind all you are grateful for. Just the fact that you woke up is amazing. A great number of people who were alive yesterday did not wake up today, and statistically more young people die per day then elders. You never know when it will be your last day, so appreciate this day. I don't say this to scare you. I point it out to show you how fortunate we are simply to be alive and able to experience all the wonders that life has to offer. When you begin and end your day with appreciation, you foster that energy to grow in your life.

Gratitude is one of the highest vibrations of energy, up there with love and joy, so you will be attuning yourself with that high vibration of energy as opposed to the lower vibrations of negativity.

Gratitude is not just something to be reserved for the good things in your life. We can be grateful for tough times as well, knowing they are opportunities for us to learn and grow. Remember that good and bad are just perceptions of mind, and we can approach both with the attitude of gratitude. We learn from everything in our lives—our mistakes and seeming negative experiences—and so we can learn to appreciate the ups and downs. What you will find happening is that the more you use the power of gratitude, this positive mind will attract more positive people and situations into your life. It's just the natural order of vibration: when you align yourself with lower vibrations of worry and negativity, you will attract more of it. And when you align yourself with the higher vibrations of gratitude and surrender, well, you see where we are going with this. Every day you have the choice to focus your mind on what you wish to experience today. You and you alone hold the awesome power to turn it all around, right at this very moment. Change your habits and truly become the conscious creator of your life.

The first step is to become mindful of what you are doing and thinking in each moment. Then shift your mind to gratitude. If you are having a difficult time feeling grateful in that moment, then try writing for five or ten minutes about the things and people you are grateful for. Try not to let your mind get hijacked and convinced by negativity. Just open your heart and mind and allow yourself to surrender to the flow of gratitude. The more you familiarize your mind with the habit of gratitude, the more you will naturally be grateful for everything in your life, and the natural flow of abundance will follow in all of its wonderful forms.

Gratitude is an abundant mind. One who has a mind of abundance truly does not *need* anything externally to fulfill them. The irony is that the external things will just start to manifest naturally because as you become content and happy, you realize that you don't really need anything. And the key to having everything is to not want anything. I am not saying external things are wrong to desire, but when you have the lack-infused mind of wanting, you only create more lack and want, because that is what you ignorantly focus on: the lack, the want. When you fill your mind with the joy of gratitude, you live as though you have all that you need. And all that you need will effortlessly show up in your life.

The Art of Joy

We have just learned why the brain goes to and clings to negative experiences. Well, the very reason it does this is because it ignorantly believes that by running these negative programs it is fostering our joy and happiness by helping us avoid pain and the possibility of even death. Ironically it brings us pain in the form of worry, anxiety, anger, fear, and so forth. We now know that this is a somewhat perverted and misguided system, so let us look at joy and how the power of joy can transform our lives. The brain wants to go to joy; it wants us to feel good and avoid suffering despite its ignorance in avoiding external suffering through inflicting us with internal mental emotional pains that deplete our ability to enjoy. Yet, it still believes it is driving us toward joy by using these negative mental states to avoid pain.

What we enjoy we will not only do time and again, but we will seek it out. This is why it is very important to bring joy to your meditation practice. Think of something you do not enjoy doing. It becomes a chore. And if you had the choice, you probably wouldn't do it. When we have this very stoic and serious attitude toward anything, it often becomes daunting, and we might force ourselves on it for a short while, but eventually we will give up. Bringing joy to our practice, however, is paramount in keeping a consistent practice. Tich Nhat Hanh, a meditation master and Zen teacher reminds us that, "if your practice does not bring you joy, you are not practicing correctly."

Although a few techniques here, especially in insight meditation, can bring us to that painful place where we must confront suppressed pains and emotions, we eventually let them go and feel more joyful and recognize that they were always bringing us a level of discomfort so we can rejoice in uprooting such inflictions of the mind. I have done much purification of negative views, and my brain does everything in its power to divert my attention from it by creating mental and physical distractions to try to keep me from looking at something painful. I even have felt like throwing up or like a burning ball of angry anxiety is looming in my solar plexus, and the brain says, "Hey, stop or you might stay like this."

Well with gaining clear insight it often takes a bit of facing painful situations, but after doing this several times I invite these practices with joy because I know the lightness and joy it brings in the long run having removed negative beliefs that lurked in my subconscious only serving to deplete the very thing we all seek, happiness and joy. The irony is that, the joy is there, the happiness is there, and these negative views serve only to cover up the joy within us, like a film on a window that we can't see through. We need to wash away those negative beliefs, and doing this with joy is key. When we sit down to practice our basic breath meditation or whatever your daily practice may be, just bring joy to mind. Note the light, joyful feeling you get when you finish your practice. We do not have to practice hard or get all heavy about it. That dramatic mind is just the workings of the survival mind. Don't force yourself to endure or push yourself to exhaustion. Our meditation should serve to allow us to express ourselves more freely, not impede or exhaust us. When I put new strings on my guitar, if they are too loose, I can't get any sound out of them, and if I wind them too tightly, they will snap and break. There is a middle ground of tuning where they sing, where I can express myself through them. Our practice and in fact our lives can be the same: not falling into the extreme of being lazy or too loose and not able to express our music like a limp string, but also not the extreme of pushing ourselves to the point that we deplete our joy and exhaust ourselves making the string so tight that it snaps. Our practice should nourish us, and although getting to the root of beliefs can often be tiresome in those practices, in the long run it nourishes us greater because we release baggage that we have unnecessarily been carrying with us for often a very long time.

Dr. Richard Davidson of the University of Wisconsin studies joy and happiness in relation to the brain. Davidson has studied the brains of monks who have spent their lives practicing meditation and positive emotions and has concluded that their happiness and joy is off the charts. This is not only a faculty reserved for monks living a monastic life, however. Davidson discovered that if any person sits quietly for a half an hour a day, meditating on compassion and kindness, that their brains will exhibit visible changes in just two weeks. Other studies have shown that people who are kind are more popular, have stronger immune systems and bodies, and are generally more successful at work. The benefits of a consistent practice are immense, and the key to a consistent practice is to bring joy to it.

Studies in neuroplasticity are proving that the brain is always being changed by the thoughts we think, the things we watch on TV or read, the people we interact with, the food we eat, and so on. We now have tools to direct that change in more positive and mindful ways, as opposed to the often unconscious change that takes place without our even being aware of it, like when we zone out and watch TV in a meditative state, allowing floods of psychological commercials to shape our brains.

Our joy resides within us, and we can train our minds to relate to it by simply becoming aware of it in everything we do. We can catch ourselves when we get caught in a dramatic or negative mind. Perhaps we are driving down the street and this happens. We can practice stopping and just becoming grateful for all we do have. We can just bring joy to the driving. Although this takes some training, especially in those who have such deep habits for negativity and drama, just realizing and seeing that we are in a negative mind state is the first step to directing it in a more positive direction.

Neuroscience is validating the amazing ability we have to change our brains and thus our lives for the better. We are living in exciting times.

The next time you sit down to practice your meditation, just reflect on that joy that is inside of you already. Even if you are in a bad mood, you can find it. Often a thought of a small child or face of a loved one is enough to allow it to arise. You can use these thoughts as points of meditation if you like, familiarizing yourself with the joy. Feel the love you have inside of you, and foster the habit of mind to readily go there. As you do this, you change the neural pathways of the brain that are carved out to go to negative, to ones that go to joy, love, and happiness. Now who wouldn't want that?

This doesn't mean that negative emotions do not arise. But as we change the habits, they do not linger for as long as they used to, because the brain now has a new habit: one that not only creates joy in our lives but in the lives of others. The mind of joy will strengthen your immune system, relieve massive amounts of unnecessary stress in your life, and create the conditions for more joy to show up in your life because what you focus on expands.

Joy and kindness go hand in hand. When you feel joyful you naturally extend kindness, and it works the other way too: being kind creates joy not only in the one we are being kind to but also in ourselves. If you get nothing else from this book, these two minds and actions will transform your life if you practice cultivating them: they are kindness and joy. Think about what that really means beyond the words. What does it mean to cultivate more joy and kindness in your life? How would your life be better if you were more able to tap into those infinite resources within you? How would it affect others in your life?

Here are a few suggestions for enforcing your habit for joy.

Create a list of five things that evoke that sense of joy in your life: It could be a child's face or an ocean wave, spending time with a loved one, anything. We can use these as points of focus to shift the mind to the immense joy we hold within us.

We can also make a list of five things we do that bring us joy. It could be playing an instrument, swimming in the ocean, spending time with family, and so forth. For me, sitting and playing my guitar helps to evoke the joy within me when I am feeling low. We can use these as points of focus or engage in them when we feel blue to help strengthen the habit of joy in our minds. Remember there is nothing outside of you that can create your joy. You are simply using these to remind you of the joy you already have within you. In any moment we can bring to mind something that evokes that joy, and joy will arise. This is proof that it is not outside of you, but a force within, and all we need do is foster a stronger relationship with it by directing the mind.

CHAPTER 13
YOU ARE THE BOSS

As we begin to cover and demystify karma, no one is responsible for your pain, your suffering, your joy, or your abundance. You are responsible for it all. You may be thinking, *Whoa, that sounds a bit rough. I didn't ask for these conditions in my life.* This may make more sense after reading the next part on karma.

The fact is that we can sit around and blame the world for our conditions. We can even blame ourselves, but none of this is constructive. Guilt is a negative mind set that serves only to take away from you and others. What we have created is already created, and wallowing in guilt, shame, or blame will not make it better. In fact, it will serve only to make things worse. You are the boss of your life. You decide if you will take action today toward empowerment or stay stuck in a backward decline of guilt. Each second is a new day, a new chance to turn it all around, so you decide in each moment.

The power of regret far outweighs the power of guilt. Regret in this sense means seeing how something causes us pain and vowing never to inflict that on any other living being. It gives us strength and empathy to not only change the conditions of our lives but those of others as well. Guilt, on the other hand, serves only to create a mind of feeling sorry for ourselves. The mind of guilt says, "I am a bad person," whereas regret looks into the past and acknowledges it and then thinks, *What can I do about it?* Here are some synonyms of guilt: *fault, blame, sin.* Here are some synonyms of regret: *repent, mourn, be sorry.* So there is no power in feeling guilty. Let us use the power of regret to move forward as opposed to the power of guilt to keep us stuck in cycles of blame. These are just words here: it's the state of mind, the way of being I am describing here.

Again, I implore you to make all of this your own, so it makes sense to your psychology and hero's journey. You are well on your way and path. Be steadfast. Don't allow back steps to deter you, for the hero journeys to discover the elixir which he or she can bring back to the people. Gain a resolve for the world, perhaps start with your loved ones: how can you be of benefit if you were more positive, joyful, and full of gen-uine love to the youth in your life, or anyone for that matter? Working on our self is selfless. The world will benefit far more from a person who is good humored, humble, and strong as opposed to anxious and angry, or whatever the circumstance.

Go forth with courage, be brave and remember: *Never give up!* Many people have the habit to give up right before the race is over, because they didn't realize they had about one percent left. Often insecurities sabotage success because they don't feel worthy. Too often we give up right before the end or before the change. Let's transform this habit and stay the course for the good of all beings. Because as Gandhi said, "We must be the change we wish to see in the world."

Equanimity

Life is a gentle cycle of ups and downs. Okay, it's often more like a rough torrent of waves swelling up and crashing down, but regardless, this is how the cycles work. If you have ever seen a graph of energy waves, it flows with an upward and downward motion. Because everything is composed of energy, naturally everything has this up-and-down cycle. This is the dualistic world we live in: inner and outer, left and right, up and down, and so forth. When we realize that they are one and the same, two sides of the same coin, it is easier for us to traverse. You can't have an up without the down. It is impossible. What would you call it? And how would you relate and know that it was up? Therefore, they are really one unit, like all the dualities in life. All just simply exist until we bring our judgment minds to the table. Our lives follow the structure of energy of which they are composed. We have ups and we have downs. In fact, our days are composed of such rhythms. We wake up have a spike of energy. Then wane down and finally retire to sleep. There is a gentle ebb and flow of all of life. The tides go up and then go back down. Notice that this is happening in all of the natural world: the moon waxes to a full then wanes down to a new. The sun rises and falls, the seasons bring birth and death, and so on. In our lives, however, we often get caught in the ups and the downs. When we are up, we cling to it, and we want it to last forever. But like all natural things, it will not, so we naturally go down. And we often vilify the down cycles in whatever form they take. So we stay in what we call a *rut*, hoping we will be up again.

This is a tiresome way of living. Equanimity simply means that we keep a calm composure in both the ups and the downs, knowing they are a natural part of life. I love the way Joseph Campbell explained this in his wonderful book *The Power of Myth*. He wrote as follows:

> In the Middle Ages a favorite image that occurs in many, many contexts is the wheel of fortune. There's the hub of the wheel, and there is the revolving rim of the wheel. For example, if you are attached to the rim of the wheel of fortune, you will be either above going down or at the bottom coming up. But if you are at the hub, you are at the same place all the time.

When we ride the hub of life, we stay centered. Wisdom rides in the center. In sports, as in life, the ups and downs happen quickly. One moment you can be scoring a goal, and the next you can be the reason the other team scores. One moment you are up, and the next you are down. All great athletes know that you have to let it go and stay centered.

I would not call myself an avid golfer, but I play every once in a while. What I found is that when I use to hit a bad shot off into the woods or water I would carry that with me to the next shot, and that one would often go astray too, further frustrating me and affecting the rest of my game. I remember once after a long trip to India and much meditation on letting go and being present, I played a game of golf with my father and brother in law. I set up to tee off on one of the holes, and sure enough I hit a terrible shot. But then I stopped, took a breath, smiled, teed up once again, and reset my swing. This next shot was spot on. I continued doing this throughout my game: whenever I would hit a bad shot. I golfed one of the best games I have ever played. We can do this in all of our lives: we can use the experiences of our mistakes to learn. We can use the seeming *negative experiences* as opportunities to reset our focus. But we don't have to cling to the ups and push away the downs. We can see that they are one and the same and just allow them to express themselves in the moment they are present, moving through them, staying centered.

When we are going through a hard time, it often seems that all we will know is this low time, as if we will never be happy again. I have been through some dark times in my life when I have questioned if there would ever again be light in my life. But of course there was. Often the problem is that we carry that down with us even when the natural cycle is coming back up. By doing this, life becomes a drag. Learning to ride the waves and tides of our lives is crucial in order to stay centered and focused, and meditation helps us immensely with this.

With equanimity we learn to stay centered and undisturbed by the negative emotions and downs in our lives. It is not that we don't feel sadness or pain ever. We don't become like a piece of Styrofoam. We just don't allow downs to destroy the balance of the mind. The term *equanimity* comes from the Latin meaning "having an even mind." In fact it is two words: *aequus*, meaning "balance" and *animus*, meaning "spirit" or "internal state." When we can learn to have an even mind in both the ups and downs of our lives, we will be more focused, centered, and full of vigor.

True equanimity produces a person who is warmhearted through thick and thin, a true leader able to traverse the path of danger and thick uncertainty as well as the sunny paths of ease. When we are truly centered, we are a force to be reckoned with. As Norman Vincent Peale once said, "The cyclone derives its powers from a calm center. So does a person."

It is important to note that equanimity does not mean to suppress. We are not looking at the negative aspects of our lives and pushing them deep down, hidden someplace with a forced smile. This is not equanimity, and this will only further disturb our inner balance. You can think of it as a form of pure love. When love is pure it loves whether the person or situation is deemed *good* or *bad*. All love knows is love. And it is gentle yet powerful. Equanimity allows the natural flow of life to express itself through you without your judgments and grasping or aversions. We learn not to suppress the negative and seeming down cycles and not to identify or cling to the ups. Just staying centered through both of them will allow us to enjoy life more.

Sounds easy enough, right? Well, here are some ways we can cultivate equanimity in our lives. Meditation is a great way to do this. As we have learned, meditation allows us to let go of our misconceptions and false views of our self and the world around us. Meditation allows us to develop that strong center and stability without being hijacked by the highs and lows. We can just notice when negative judgments enter our minds and practice letting them go in all situations in our lives. For example, if we are going to do some event or see someone we rather wouldn't, negative mental states usually arise, and we begin the judgment cycle. We can practice replacing them with acceptance and loving-kindness.

We think we know everything there is to know about a person or situation, when in truth we don't. People and things are changing all the time. So by staying in a mental state of "I don't know" and having an open heart and mind helps immensely.

Perhaps someone irritates us. We can bring to mind their suffering and realize they just want to be happy. We then can walk the middle ground, not getting caught in their neurosis and reacting and not pushing them away and being repulsed. We can stop and accept the negative judgments and emotions and allow them to just pass through without suppressing it or grasping at it. We can then replace it with wisdom. If we are mindful of a situation like this, we will notice that our mind and body becomes tense. We can simply practice relaxing the tension. The tension will arise again because we are in the habit of tensing up in these situations but we can just observe this and practice letting it go. Once we can cultivate a relaxed state we can begin to adapt an attitude of welcoming the person or situation as opposed to resisting them. We open with love and allow the person or situation to be what it is without trying to control or resist. We can do this with every situation in our lives, learning to live and surf the waves of life and learning to enjoy. What you will find is that the quality of your life will increase, you will become more open and loving and a symbol of strength and solidarity to all you interact with. Life becomes more enjoyable when we learn to accept the ups and downs for what they are and simply live.

Generosity of the Heart

In the United States, where I currently sit and write this, we have many different structures of wealth and lack thereof. From the very poor to the very rich and in between, for the most part those of us who have a computer, smart phone or even a basic cellular phone are pretty well off in respect to many other places in the world, including right here in the United States. Although it is important to practice giving monetarily as well as gifts of physical nature, we often have problems cultivating gifts from the heart and sometimes even with receiving them. What are gifts from the heart you may ask? One need not give only money or other gifts, but a heartfelt compliment or even a hug to someone you would not otherwise even think to give one to can generate a massive well of wealth and kindness from not only the receiver but the giver as well. Search yourself; is there any hindrance in telling someone what they mean to you or expressing your gratitude for them in your life? Too often I hear stories of those who have lost loved ones or friends, and they regret not having said certain things to them while they were alive. Who in your life have you wanted to give a gift from the heart but didn't? Often it's our ego, our worry about what others think, that impedes us from shining our warmth from the heart. Yet, even a simple *thank you* or expression of love or gratitude can completely shift someone's day around and often his or her life.

I have noticed that we often have trouble paying someone a compliment or telling him or her what we think deep down in our hearts. I remember times of going out with some buddies of mine, and they would pour their hearts out with how much we meant to each other as close friends, like brothers, while the truth serum of alcohol was high in the mind. Yet it's discursive from the normality of our sober days, and often not as valid as when one says it truly from a place of integrity of mind and body.

I have also found, myself included, that we have trouble receiving gifts of the heart from others. When others pay us a compliment, we often fire one right back without even allowing it to settle in. In effect, we aren't allowing the other to give, which upsets the natural flow of give and take that governs our natural world: like the tides that rise and fall or the breath that inhales and exhales. Next time someone compliments you, try a simple and genuine, "Thank you". Allow it to settle, and resonate with your heart. Doing this you not only generate a habit and unconscious memory to relate to yourself as this positive affirmation the other has given you, but also you are allowing the other to give to you as well as strengthening your habit to receive.

Numerous studies have shown that the simple act of giving and receiving boosts serotonin levels and strengthens the immune system, and more so in the giver. A study by psychologists at the University of British Columbia noted that children had higher increases in happiness when giving than when receiving. What I found interesting is that it was reported that not only the giver and receiver experience boosts of serotonin and improved immune system functions, but also any witnesses of those giving experience this as well!

A Harvard University study called this phenomenon the Mother Teresa Effect. Researchers took 132 Harvard students and measured the level of Immunoglobin A present in their saliva. Immunoglobin A is a crucial antibody in the immune system. They then had the students watch a film about Mother Teresa's work among the poor people of Calcutta, India. After the film they again measured the level of Immunoglobin A present in their saliva. The results were that all of those who watched the film had increased levels of Immunoglobin A just by simply observing someone else doing charity work. What's more is that studies showed that those who regularly engage in charitable work or acts of kindness experience alleviation from chronic pains, stress, and insomnia.

A smile at a stranger at the store can result in thousands of more smiles throughout the day. I remember once, in a funk, I was walking down a busy New York City street, and someone had genuinely smiled at me in passing, prompting me to smile. I could feel a noticeable increase in serotonin and had lifted my head a bit more and kept a smile on my face that extended to many others as I walked the street. That person could have in effect created ten thousand or more smiles and increased the immunity of others with a simple smile. Now think of the power of that as it spreads to the entire world! After all, we are all an interconnected network of energy.

Now that we have looked at the research and science of how generosity can have amazing physical and mental benefits on not only the giver and receiver but the observer of such acts as well, let's look into our hearts and see where there may be blocks.

For those who may be emotionally closed off, start with your family.

Perhaps you can send a heartfelt text or pick up the phone and tell someone you love them or appreciate them. The next time you are on a busy line at the store, perhaps you let someone go in front of you. The possibilities are endless. And when you bring joy into this process you will double the serotonin and immunity function.

There have been many stories of those who have realized enlightenment through generosity. The Chinese Hoi Tai, also known as the laughing Buddha, often depicted as a plump, jolly man bearing gifts, is one such representation of this. Saint Nicholas, also known as Santa Claus, is another depiction of an enlightened saint who had realized enlightenment through giving.

Cultivate generosity by giving from the heart, not only physically but emotionally. Be an ear of compassion, give a shoulder to lean on, give your time to someone who loves you. We can give a dollar to someone on the street without conjuring up our stories of them such as, "Oh they must be an alcoholic," and so forth. The fact is that if someone is pleading for pocket change they suffer immensely, so it's an opportunity for you to not only strengthen the habit of generosity in your mind but also to help another living being on whatever level that may be in the moment. Keep in mind that every time we don't want to give we are closing the door to receiving.

We can cultivate the mind of giving while paying our bills. We have to pay them, so we might as well be happy about it and cultivate habits of joy and giving for future joy and receiving. Be creative! There are so many opportunities to cultivate generosity and giving in your life every day. Learn to be as excited to give as you get when you receive and watch your entire world change.

Studies show that people who are kind and generous are more popular than those who are not. When you learn to put others first and cultivate giving, people are naturally attracted to you, and you raise the vibration of the world.

PART 2

Action and Intention, Sowing the seeds for a New Garden

Within the pages of this book, we have been looking at techniques to help us move through destructive emotions bred by thoughts and views, without getting stuck in them and relating to them as being inherently who we are. Remember, even a beautiful lotus grows out of the mud. So we are using the undesirable situations and habits in our lives and transforming them, rising out of them like the lotus from the mud. These methods we have learned are to be practiced for the long haul and to be made your own, tailored and structured to how you best relate to them so they work for you. Many just leave them as is; some change them slightly; and others take what works and incorporate them into the system I teach here in ways that create extraordinary change.

In these next sections, we will be learning how to change those destructive habit energies from ones that disempowered us to ones that empower us. Within this structure we can be using the techniques from Part 1 of this series combined with the ones we will learn here in Part 2. We will be rewiring the brain in order to attract more love, abundance, joy, or whatever it is we wish to attract into our lives. We begin first with our motives or intentions for doing so.

CHAPTER 14
INTENTION

Our intentions here are pretty clear: to create habits of mind that lead to more joy, abundance, love, and so forth. Intention is important. It is what sets in motion everything that proceeds from it. Intention is so powerful because with our intentions, our motivations, our lives can be changed right here, right now, simply by changing the intentions behind what we do. We are using intention all of the time: when I lift my arm, it comes from my mind telling it to. If I think, *Shake my head,* the body follows the mind. Most of our intentions are unconscious and unclear. A simple intentional habit such as lifting my arm to shake someone's hand does not have to be thought about in depth. It's reactionary and quick, but so are many others that create harmful actions out of reaction.

Take a moment to review your intentions. It is wise to look at your intentions in all you do. What is my intention for meditating today? What is my intention for eating this or doing that? Asking that simple question will have a profound effect on what follows. We can simply create an intention to love our lives: this simple shift can have amazing effects on our daily lives. Intention changes everything. Whatever mind we enter into a situation with helps create the situation for us. Our intentions craft the world around us.

In sorcery and magic, intention is a powerful tool that all good sorcerers use to their advantage. When you hear of white and black magic, the simple understanding of what separates the two is as follows. Black magic is something done with a selfish intention: gaining things or situations for the self alone, not taking into account others and the whole of existence. White magic is something done with a selfless intention, for the benefit of others. One is done at the cost of others; the other in benefit of others. We can demystify magic here knowing that we are all creating sorcery in our lives. The problem is that we are not usually conscious of it. The intentions are on autopilot, and much of the time they are creating black magic from a fight-or-flight, primordial mind of separation. As we learn to become more mindful sorcerers, we learn that behind every thought and action lies an intention. We can work on ourselves to be of benefit to all. We can eat an apple for others. That apple will nourish us and allow us to be of the greatest benefit of all. This view may seem quixotic, but I assure you it will transform your life with strength, wisdom, and endless abundance because you are now training the mind in the truth of our interconnection, moving from the selfish and ignorant view to the one that we are all in this together. Nothing is impossible because you are all possibilities. The wisest of masters were the greatest of sorcerers. They could create whatever they wanted in their lives. Yet, all of them taught us that if we serve others, our own needs will be fulfilled, because all we are is other. The experience of this comes only in living it. The intellectual mind may grasp the concept, but the power lies in living this.

We don't often really know our intentions and blindly go about our lives following our unconscious, habitual mind. Often the intention may not be the best. If your intention for eating a box of Twinkies is to avoid the pain of a recent breakup, then at least you understand why you are doing it, and even if you engage in that box of Twinkies, your clear seeing will eventually move you away from these destructive habits. As you apply what we have just learned, you will rapidly help change the reactive habits, using wisdom and compassion: wisdom, meaning to see things clearly for what they are and taking into account that there is a process you need to go through, being compassionate toward yourself within each step of that process. Not judging even what you may view as the most vial and guilt ridden actions you perform. Change is not only possible it is what is happening constantly. With the proper intentions you are empowering yourself for a better life ahead to live, as Neale Donald Walsch puts it, "the grandest version of the greatest vision you ever had about yourself."

Intention Vs. Expectation

Often we become confused between an expectation and an intention. Allow me to give you some clarity into the differences between the two. Here are the dictionary definitions of the two:

Expectation: *A strong belief that someone will or should achieve something.*

Intention: *A thing intended; an aim or plan.*

When we have an expectation, we are building a scenario in our mind that rarely comes true. If it does, it almost never comes true the way we envisioned it . If it doesn't come true, we are left forlorn, uneasy, often even angry because we have become attached to an outcome that never came into fruition. If it does come true, it almost never lives up to the expectation we have built in our heads, and we are still left upset on some level.

An intention is different, in that it is a plan or aim. Yet we can have an intention and then detach from the outcome and simply do the best we can and enjoy each step of the ride. In this way we become flexible and more open minded, and chances are it may be better than our expectation. But if we hold a strong belief that it should be this way or that, then when it shows up another way, even possibly in a way that is better for you, we get upset.

General Dwight D. Eisenhower said it best, "I have always found that plans are useless, but planning is indispensable." An intention is that act of planning, the act of aiming, but an expectation is the fool-hearted notion that it must be this way no matter what. Many a war has been lost using this notion, at the expense of entire battalions.

Living in expectation causes much suffering and worry. When you are living in expectation, you are attached to the outcome. In reality, all you can do is give one hundred percent and then surrender to what the outcome is. It does not mean you have to settle, it simply means not attaching to the outcome. Like an archer trying to hit his target, if the archer aims for the bull's eye and comes a few inches away, expectation would not only cloud his shot with worry but also sway him from the next shot with further frustration. Yet his intended target can again be aimed at and measured up, and the previous shot is now a gauge for the next. Expectation often causes much frustration, and many give up on a goal as a result. When we don't fulfill expectations, we become angry because anger arises when attachment does not get what it wants, like a child who wants a toy at the store. We have these expectations that rarely come true the way we expect them to, and so anger arises, and we suppress that anger because we know that as adults we can't pout and roll on the floor crying like a child. The suppression of our sadness and anger lead to physical pains and emotional turmoil within. As you can see, our attachments to our expectations carry heavy burdens to both our physical and psychological selves.

From a standpoint of manifesting, when we are attached to the outcome of a situation, it is less likely for it to come into fruition. Yet, when we set the aim and let it go, the chances of it happening are much more likely, because worry, fear, and attachment are not as strong. The master warrior knows that expectation is a weakness of his opponent and that intention is strength. When a river flows it has an intended path, yet it often hits rocks or a fallen tree, and thus it quickly flows around these. Imagine if rivers stopped at every rock that got in the way, stubbornly sticking to the expected path it thought it was going to tread. I picture the world's water supply to be held up at some boulder someplace: an absurd and laughable thought because expectation is unnatural. Like a tree that intends to grow straight up to the sun, often it needs to twist and turn around obstacles, and usually reaches its goal.

I am reminded of a Dr. Seuss tale about two characters walking from different directions toward each other. When they met head to head, each one refused to move because that was each character's expected path of travel. Stubbornly each stood for years as the world was building all around them in wonder. Neither would budge, fixed to their expected path. Yet, all one had to do was move over or step to the side and keep walking a slightly different path, and they too would have reaped the benefits of the wonders all around them. Yet, their ignorance kept them locked in the attachment of their expectations, and so they stayed right there, in anger, not moving until the other had because they were attached and inflexible.

Expectations are unreasonable. We never know what is going to happen tomorrow or in the next minute for that matter, and to think we can know an absolute of an outcome is an extreme mind set and unrealistic. An intention, however, gives us the freedom to create, the flexibility to traverse, and the ability to enjoy whatever comes our way without attachment to the outcome.

Think about some goals you have. Are you attached to the outcomes? What feelings arise because of those attachments? Do they make you feel tight, nervous, or worrisome?

Finally, often our intentions are unclear or we don't really know our intentions. It is wise to have an intention or think, as I said earlier, *What are my intentions for doing this?*

In this way, we bring mindfulness into our every action. We shift from reckless and irresponsible actions without intention, which usually leave us stuck in the mud, to ones that empower us to help ourselves and others. We swiftly move forward to a joyful life.

What's that Smell? Our Stinky Limitations

Using no way as way and having no limitation as limitation. ~ Bruce Lee

A great teacher of mine once used this analogy to describe our self-imposed limitations. He said that it is as if we have rotten sandwiches in our backpacks and we are walking around all day wondering, *What is that smell?*

We go to school, work, everywhere, and there it is again: that putrid smell. *Everywhere I go that same nasty smell,* we think. Finally we realize that the smell is coming from our backpack. We thought we kept going places where the smell was, but what we were doing was bringing the smell with us wherever we went. It is like that with our limitations, the sandwich represents the limited self we view, the limitations we bring to our relationships, our jobs, everywhere. We first have to realize that we are bringing this limitation into all we do, we are creating this.

We have just learned how to find and recognize the smell in our proverbial backpacks and now, once we remove the rotten sandwich, we may have to wash out the bag, because it's still smelly. Then we can put something in that smells more desirable or doesn't smell at all. In essence, as we transform and change our negative habitual emotions, when we learn to stop allowing them to control us, we stop relating to them as who we are because they are just a view we have from the past, a deluded and wrong view, a fantasy we have conjured up based on the past that is influencing the present moment. As we do this, soon they become less and less powerful. So in a sense, we are removing the energy that destroys our desirable outcomes. Sometimes the habit energy will show up again after doing the work, but now it yields almost no power over our actions: if it does we now have clear insight into it and know how to quickly diffuse it.

We now will learn how to create desirable habits by understanding how we created the habits and outcomes we currently have. We will soon see that we hold the key to creating the habits we desire to have in order to live more abundant and joyful lives.

In this book we have been investigating how our views lead to thoughts, which lead to actions or inaction, fight, flight, or freeze. Often we are paralyzed by views of our past and very often this is what impedes us from the life we wish to live. We need to stop relating to the limited views we have about ourselves, recognizing that those limits are based on past events or thoughts that are not who we are now. As we start relating more and more to the limitless self, which is always changing, we can then begin to embrace the fact that anything is possible for us in that space of limitless opportunity. We begin to take our narrow view of the world, this deluded view that we are stuck and fixed, and we open it up to the true reality, which is the broad view of our limitless nature.

As you begin to experience this, life starts to become much more enjoyable and fulfilling. You begin to change in ways you never thought possible, and as you change your life in a more positive direction, you will begin to influence the world in a more positive direction.

CHAPTER 15
ACTION, REACTION

In the ancient language of Sanskrit the word *karma* translates as "action." We hear this word *karma* very often in our Western modern world. It has become synonymous with New Age culture, and more often than not is misunderstood. Karma is the key factor in creating a life of abundance, joy, love, and really whatever you wish to experience. Karma teaches us how to act in order to experience what we wish to experience. Many of us have vision boards or use manifestation techniques, with little or no result. What started as an exciting venture of creating our lives, often ends with frustration and doubt.

Karma is the key factor in creating what we want in our lives. This is the science that we will use to create what we want to show up, now that we have learned to disengage and clear out the old karmic habits.

For whatsoever a man soweth, that shall he also reap. ~ Galatians 6:7

According to Newton's Third Law or Law of Motion, every action creates an equal and opposite reaction. Every time we think or act, we are creating a cause. And in time those thoughts and actions will have an effect. Therefore everything we say, do, and think in life is a karma (action) and leaves an imprint on the mind. Consequently, the result of that action will follow in time. Everything we are currently experiencing is a result of an action from the past. When we create an action, it sets into motion a series of reactions and consequences that echo out into the world, which leaves an imprint on our minds. Once we set into motion an action, we will undoubtedly reap what we sow. This is not some punishment or gift from a far off God, it's simply a matter of cause and effect. It is as if we toss a large rock up into the sky. From the point of view of punishment, someone would catch the rock and throw it down onto our heads. From the karmic standpoint, when you throw a rock up, it must come down, according to natural law, and when it does it could strike you in the head if you are not mindful of your previous action of tossing a stone in the air. As Robert Green Ingersoll said, "In nature there are neither rewards nor punishments; there are consequences."

Karma is not some heavy concept that happens only when really good or very bad things show up, it is a result of every second we are alive. Eating a cookie is a karma, the action of eating a cookie creates memory and that memory or imprint creates desire, or aversion depending on whether or not we liked the cookie. This desire or aversion prompts another action, and so we are now creating neural pathways in the brain, like computer software. We are wiring our brains with our actions every second, and unfortunately we have become bundles of unconscious wiring. As a result, we are often mindless, reactive machines who base our behavior on unconscious choices structuring our brains.

We have become a series of unconscious reactions based on past actions and often feel like we have been dealt a bad hand in life, but we not only dealt those cards to ourselves we also set each card that we received in our hand. Mostly, we have done this unconsciously, and therefore it feels like the luck of the draw. We make choices unconsciously, based on actions of the past, caught in an unconscious tailspin or action reaction. Your future is created by the choices you make every second. A good example is if you woke up and stubbed your toe. This now sets into motion a series of reactions and actions due to the energy of that stubbed toe. If we just allow ourselves to stop, we can allow that energy to run through us instead of holding onto it in the form of reactions. Many times something like a stubbed toe is easily let go, but other things are not, in our lives.

Karma is analogous to an accounting program. The universe has a flawless accountant that makes sure no debt goes unpaid. All gets balanced. Often we do a good deed or see people do very bad things and wonder, *Why has that person not experienced that negative karma back?* With each action we plant a seed, and like a seed in a field, when the conditions are right for it to start growing, it will. With patience and acceptance and the understanding of how karma works, we can surrender to the moment, knowing all we need to do in that moment is be kind and enjoy. We don't have to be the karma police, watching carefully for the seeds to ripen for ourselves or others. This would be an expectation, and often karma ripens in ways our expectations could not fathom. Surrender to the process, and live in each moment as it passes, knowing that being kind and enjoying all you do not only makes that moment with you and others better, but also creates the karma for others to be kind to you. More joy will follow because you are creating the habit for kindness and joy.

Never Judge Karma

When it comes to karma, try to never get heavy about it, because it is just as it is. To get heavy is to create drama, which is exactly what the survival, fight-or-flight mind eats up. We tend to like drama in our culture. It seems that everywhere we turn there it is: the news is very good at creating drama with real life situations. Things are as they are, and to get heavy and dramatic about them only makes worse a situation and can blow a good situation out of proportion and dull the actual experience of it. Remember that we are creating our karma in each second we breathe. So, how wonderful! Nothing to get heavy about, because if we don't like it, then we know how to change it.

Try to remember never to judge others' karma because what may seem like positive or negative karma may not actually be what it appears to be. For example, you may see a man with millions of dollars and think, *He must have good karma*, yet his money could be his negative karma. It may keep him in constant worry of losing it and in a state of miserliness to hold onto it. This may not be true as well. It may well be his positive karma, but one never knows. Conversely, we can see a man who is poor, and this can be his positive karma. I once knew a man who had millions of dollars, and it was the source of his misery and pain in many ways. And I have met a man who had no money and was one of the happiest and most joyful people I have ever met. I have also met people in poverty who were not so happy, and many very happy wealthy people, but you get the point here.

A good friend of mine developed cancer in her lung, which spread elsewhere in her body. The doctors didn't think she had much time to live. It would seem that she had some negative karma, yet she overcame the cancer and went into remission and she gained a new insight into life, one that put her on a path to help others and give them hope for survival. She still until this day touches the lives of many, and she will be the first one to tell you that the cancer was one of the best things that ever happened to her. Although when she was in the thick of it, we were all scared, and she probably didn't think so at the time, but in hindsight it was obvious. Even if someone gets sick and dies, it could have been exactly what they needed to let something go and elevate their path. The point is, we never know, and so to judge karma is a foolish thing to do. A very wise man once told me, "To know is not to know, not to know is to know." Socrates said it best, "The only thing I know is that I know nothing at all." Often we feel we know everything about someone or something, but the truth is that we have no idea.

Mindful Action (Karma), The Power to Create

Here we will get into the meat and potatoes of creation. You will find that the answer to creating what you want in life is not as difficult as you would think. As we learned earlier, karma is the key factor in creation and manifesting, for the simple fact that we reap what we sow. Our actions have reactions and are responsible for what shows up in our lives. So wouldn't it be wise to be mindful of those actions and keep them in line with the pure intentions in our lives?

If, for example, we wish to create wealth in our lives, then we create the causes for wealth by practicing generosity with the right intention. The ignorance of greed and miserliness is that it thinks in order to be wealthy, in order to have more money and material things, then we need to hold onto what we have. The wisdom is that to create more money, we must give it away. We must create it for others. Remember, all we are is other, so when we create this for them, we are becoming the source of it. There is a natural give and take in the world, an ebb and flow. Things must be given and taken in order for life to exist. Like a tree that gives oxygen and the animals that give it carbon dioxide, the symbiotic exchange is crucial to their biological survival. Breathing is the basic example of this: when you inhale, you must exhale in order to bring in more oxygen, or else you die. If you want something in your life, become the source of it: if you want love, create love in others' lives. If you want money and abundance, create it for others. This is the simple wisdom that we will look at more deeply to see how we can actually live by this.

You may be saying, "Well this is great, but I don't even have a dollar for myself let alone to give someone else." This is where we can become creative. The mind creates value in terms of the intentions we place on the actions we take. For example, we can feed birds crumbles of bread and think in our minds that with this bread we are feeding the entire world: the mind is limitless and will register this experience. It's the brain that creates limit and doubt. We can give a dollar to a homeless person and envision that we are giving money to every needy person. We can imagine we are giving abundance to the world. By creating the inward experience, we are creating new habits in the mind of giving and generosity and creating the karma for wealth and abundance in our lives. At first it may be about us, what we will get back in return, and many think this is not the way to go about this. But often this is a necessary step in the process. What you will find is that something interesting begins to happen. We begin to enjoy the process of giving, and soon it becomes more about giving and less about what we will get in return. This is where the real magic begins to happen.

Many athletes use visualization to reach the goals they set. The reason this is such a successful method with those such as Olympic athletes is because the brain does not know the difference between what you visualize and what you actually do. When one Olympic runner was observed during her hurdling visualization, the observers found in their tests that the same muscles were firing as if she were actually running the race. The body and mind think she is actually running the race, and the beauty is that she is running the perfect race in her head, creating the habit for success out on the track.

The point is that we can begin to use the awesome power of the mind in our lives every day, by creating the intentions for generosity with a big mind. Even if we perceive what we are giving is small, we can change our perceptions. We can learn to rejoice in the abundance and love of others as opposed to feeling jealous or sad that we don't have what they have. When we rejoice in the good fortune of others, we are taking part in their good fortune and creating that habit for ourselves as opposed to feeling separate and forlorn or jealous, which only serves to create more lack because we are creating the habit for more jealousy, more separation, and forlorn situations to occur in our lives. Rejoicing in the good fortune of others, we enter into the stream of their good fortune. And when we rejoice in our good fortune, we expand it: the opposite is also true. When we change our mind, we change our world. We must learn to become the source of what we desire to show up in our lives. In the next few sections we will look at how we can do this.

CHAPTER 16
RECREATING OUR GARDENS

Like any good gardener, we begin to enjoy the process of gardening and we naturally enjoy the fruits of our labor. In fact, we will bear more fruit as a result of our joyful gardening. As we just learned, when we become the source of what we wish to experience in our lives, not only do we create the causes and conditions for it to show up in our lives, but we begin to enjoy creating it in others' lives.

Here are a few examples of other ways we can do this.

If we wish to have a fulfilling and loving relationship in our lives but do not currently, then many times when we see others who do have this, jealousy comes up. We may seem happy for them on the outside, but inside somewhere we are teeming with jealousy and resentment that they have what we desire. Instead we can go inside, use the techniques from part one where we discussed stopping to allow the emotion to pass through and delving in to see why we react in such ways, and then begin to truly feel happy for them. When we are genuinely joyful for others' wealth, abundance, and love, then we are sharing in it and creating the causes for this to show up in our lives, because the mind now relates to already having it. As we rejoice in the good fortune of others we create the habit to have more of it in our lives, as opposed to the delusional view of lack that rears its head in the form of jealousy, anger, pride, and so forth. We can do this with anything, and everything. Think about something you would like to have in your life now and creatively use this technique to retrain the mind that perceives lack to realize you already have it, because as we will soon see, we do.

We can pay our bills with a positive mind that creates more abundance. Often when we pay our bills we get upset, *Bills bills bills!* we think. In the United States we have more personal debt than ever before. This over-whelms us and creates the mind of lack, a negative net worth. We are so fortunate to even be able to have institutions to lend us this money. That alone can be our immense positive karma. In other parts of the world, the scenario often goes something like this: you work a fifty-hour week to barely scrape by and feed your family and pay your rent (as it is here often as well). Yet, if you lose your job or if you can't afford food, that's it. There is no credit for you to receive, you just don't eat. For the most part, we are very abundant and do not even realize it. So what can we do the next time we pay bills? Realize that the money has to keep flowing, like the blood in our veins: if it stops up, a disease or problematic situation will arise. Pay the bills with joy, replace the heavy-hearted anger of paying out all this money to one of joy to even be able to pay. Even in paying our bills we can create the causes for future wealth.

Remember, we can do this with any situation in our lives. If we wish for more wisdom in our lives, create more wisdom in the lives of others. Be creative, be steadfast, but most important, do it. Remember to apply patience, because it often takes time to create a new habit, and sometimes takes time for what you wish to show up to show up. Often we quit right before it comes, like running a marathon and quitting at the last few hundred feet because we don't see the finish line yet and we get frustrated. Just as a beautiful flower takes time to grow and blossom, there is a process and all in the right time. You have been unconsciously creating much of what you do not want to show up in your life. So isn't it well worth the patience and application of new habits in your mind to eventually be living the life you are meant to live in order to be of the greatest good to all? Remember, working on our self is a selfless endeavor because the world will benefit from a generous, kind-hearted, and joyful individual more than it will from an angry, jealous, and miserly one.

The Secret Key to Manifesting
Our inner GPS is throwing us off

Manifesting what we wish to experience in life is not as hard as it seems. In fact, as we have just learned, this is what we are doing all the time. Within this book, we are looking at skillful ways of creating the life we wish to manifest for the greater good of not only ourselves but of all those around us. Remember that when we become the source of what we want, we create the energy and wisdom within us that we are not separate from this, and it shows up in our lives. This is, however, often easier said and read than done.

Many of us have created vision boards and used positive thinking and affirmation, only to find that what we were focused on never came to fruition. This is frustrating and causes us to question ourselves and our beliefs. The reason this most often happens is because although we are thinking and looking at what we want, we are still allowing the deluded mind to drive us. It is like we get in a car in New York and wish to drive to Florida, which is south of New York. We put pictures up all over the car of beautiful Florida sunsets and the like. We keep thinking, *Florida, Florida, Florida,* but our internal GPS tells us to drive north, toward Maine. We can focus on the pictures and thoughts all we want, but our actions are coming from the wrong place: our GPS is misguiding us. Well, our internal GPS of fear, anger, greed, craving, jealousy, and so on misguide us all the time. And unfortunately we follow it even when our intention was to go someplace else. We can have the great intention of being kind and never harming others, but our GPS of anger will surely confuse us, and if we follow it, we create much harm with our actions and words.

Our intention of being wealthy because we wish to do great deeds with our wealth is great. We may have an intended path even clearly laid out to get there, but our GPS may be misguiding us with fear and so we create all these excuses of why this would never work out and how we should just quit and do something else. These delusions are very convincing to us. We can go on and on with examples like this, and I am sure you can see examples of this in your own life.

I am about to offer simple manifesting steps based on all that we have been learning, and hopefully practicing. When we learn to stop following the broken system of our GPS, we create a new GPS system of the heart that overrides all fears and delusions, and we begin to *feel the fear and do it anyway.* We learn to not be slaves to the directions of our delusions and rise above and take the high road toward our truth, not the delusions' cloudy and insecure truth based on fear and ignorance.

Here is a good method to recognize and move past the grip of our delusional fears that impede us from experiencing what we intend to experience. Break out your goal list and dust off your vision boards because this is going to prove to be the missing key, the secret that makes it all possible.

Steps to Manifesting

Step 1 – Gain Clarity and Locate the Blocks:

Before you even begin the creation process, take a moment to look at the intention behind it and gain some clarity into exactly what it is you wish to experience. Then you can sit and clear your mind for a moment, using any method that works for you, be it some deep breathing or a breath ratio that we learned earlier or any of the techniques that you have been using. After a few moments, bring to mind what you wish to create and just observe any negative views or emotions that come up. Use the powerful words "I am (fill in the blank)," if you like, and simply observe if there is any fear in the form of greed, anger or jealousy. Depending on what you are looking to create, there will be different delusions for different situations. Obviously, you must learn to feel them, and words can't ever explain experience, so we learn to feel the energies and we will know the blocked energy emotion when we feel it. Then we trace it to a thought or thoughts. What are the impeding views you have about this? If you are looking to create more money in your life, do you vilify money? Perhaps you have the twisted view that spiritual people do not need money or it makes them bad. What beliefs have you been conditioned to think? These often come up from our parents or teachers, friends, or media. At this point, just recognizing the impeding energy that conflicts with what we want is enough to move on to the next step. For example, if we wish to create a job where we are an artist, fears may arise such as "What if I am a failure, what if I can't make money, what will others think of me?" These are enough to take us off the path toward what we wish to create in our life. Taking steps to do what we want in life doesn't have to be fool-hearted and sloppy, but to do nothing and never follow what our heart wishes is the most fool-hearted of all.

When I wanted to go off and become a writer, I still had a full-time job, and I saved money and kept my goals in mind, all the while noticing that nagging fear that told me I may fail, that I am crazy for leaving a full time job to do something I have no idea what the outcome may be. The list went on, but I drove the car. My heart drove, and I took steps to ultimately do what I love to do. We can all skillfully drive the cars of our lives. What we want to manifest may not happen as quickly as we like. In fact, it may take a long time, but we will never achieve the goal or create what we want if we let the delusion drive us. If I had listened to that fear all those years ago, I would still have the dream of writing, traveling, and teaching, but would have never left my job and my dreams would have stayed dreams. Action is the most important part here: clear action from the heart, from you, not from the fear-driven mind. We can do this with anything: if we wish to manifest a loving relationship, we can sit and bring it to mind and see what comes up. Perhaps thoughts come up of not being good enough, or fears arise that we will never find someone we like or who likes us. Our actions spawn from those fears. We don't approach someone on the street who smiled at us, in fear of rejection. Fear has driven us away. Simply just keeping that fear in the mind is enough to blind us from the opportunities all around us. In this step we are observing the impeding emotions that block us from our goals and intentions and using wisdom if we wish to dismantle them, as we have been learning.

Step 2 – Dissolve and Replace:

Allow the fear, greed, craving, or whatever the negative emotion to dissipate. Like in the laboratory meditation, just breathe it away, realizing that we are creating it with our mind. We are sitting perfectly safe from any danger, just entertaining an idea. There is no need for the negative emotion. It is just a thought. Just a view from the past, so we let it pass through us. When we are again clear and calm and in that space of creation, we can visualize what we wish to manifest, just allowing ourselves to feel the emotions of having it. Get excited as if you already have it, feel it, bring it to life. This creates a neural pathway in our brains for the experience.

Remember the story of the Olympic Hurdler who visualized the perfect race in her head every day? Well she was creating neural pathways for success, and the experience of having what she wanted. This is exactly what we are doing here.

"Therefore I say to you, all things for which you pray and ask, believe that you have received them, and they will be granted you." Mark 11:24. This wonderful passage gives us clarity into a key component to manifesting. As we have been learning our beliefs and the thoughts spawned by those beliefs are what create our reality. If we are telling ourselves we are a millionaire and a little voice in our head says, "Yeah right you're a broke loser," then we need to deal with that little voice, that belief that holds us back from manifesting what we wish to experience in life.

Step 3 – Act As If:

This step happens on our meditation break: our everyday lives which are the most beneficial part of our meditations. Now we create actions that will bring us closer to our goals. We can take small steps every day, with a never-give-up attitude. We can feel the fear and do it anyway, with the wisdom that the fears are just fantastic stories. We can get inspired by those who have been successful and realize that if one person can do it so can we. Many overcome intense odds to be successful in achieving goals. There are no excuses except the excuses you create. Remember, there are only opportunities to learn and grow. Keep in mind that when we become the source of something for others and when we rejoice in others' good fortune, we are taking part in it and creating the neural pathways in our brain and experience of already being successful or having it. If we wish to have more money, we can become more generous. Even if we feel greed and fear that we don't even have a dollar to give, we can give it. Or we can feed the ducks with a big mind, visualizing that the duck food is feeding the entire world. You direct the mind, and the mind will believe you once you recognize the disempowering views. Like sitting in a chair and envisioning a hurdle race, the same muscles fired on that Olympic runner as if she were running the race. The mind doesn't know the difference. If you wish to create a loving relationship in your life, rejoice in others who currently have one in their lives. Note the jealousy that comes up, yet don't allow yourself to be hijacked by it. Remember, do not suppress the jealousy. You can write it out until you are clear and then wisely and clearly learn to rejoice and feel happy for those who are in love.

Take risks that you wouldn't otherwise take in the past. Oftentimes our minds of worry reason why we shouldn't, and we listen. Perhaps there is a person you would love to talk to who smiled at you, but your anxious worry rationalizes why you shouldn't. So in the past you just avoid this situation even though you would love to date. Feel that fear, and muster up the courage to smile back or go over and strike up a conversation. Perhaps you want to ask your boss for that raise that has been long overdue, but your insecure mind that didn't feel worthy kept you from asking. All of these methods can be creatively used to create opportunities in your life. As Emerson once said, "Don't be too timid and squeamish about your actions. All life is an experiment. The more experiments you make the better." Your boss may say no, that woman who smiled at you may have a boyfriend, but if you never ask, you will never know. And as you strengthen your habit of confidence, these situations will become easier to deal with and opportunity now more abundant. Taking action and seizing moments in life is great, but remember that we must create the conditions in life for wealth, love, and joy in order to prosper. So rejoice in others' good fortune; create good fortune for others; and take action. Now you are beginning to create the conditions for the things you wish to experience to show up in your life. Be creative because you can do this with anything in your life. And don't forget Step 4, which is crucial.

Step 4 – Surrender:

This may be one of the most important steps, and it involves letting go. When we surrender in faith, we allow the natural course of life to express itself through us. The path of least resistance. It takes time to change a habit; it takes time for a seed to grow so once you plant it, have the patience and faith that it knows when and how to grow. It doesn't need you to watch it or aid it by pulling on it. In fact, this will break the seed's fruits and impede it to grow, because if you are acting in that way you don't truly believe it will happen. Go back to Step 1 if you find yourself doing this. In fact cycling through these steps will ensure your success. Taking action as in Step 3 can be done through least effort. We don't force situations to occur. We simply seize them when they arise. We recognize when they are there. We don't fret and run around all day forcing opportunities. We notice them when they show up and seize the moment.

Put simply the steps are as follows:

1. Gain Clarity and Locate the Blocks

2. Dissolve and Replace

3. Act As If

4. Surrender

CHAPTER 17
CONTROL AND THE ART OF SURRENDER

Giving up our control and surrendering to life is often one of the toughest things to do. I notice that when I do surrender and let go, my life seems to flow and even projects I am working on just seem to come together and go straight to the intended goal. Like a rock that is dropped into the water, it is in a state of complete surrender and quickly finds its way to the riverbed. It isn't consumed with thought and worries about how it's going to get there or when, or struggling against the gravity that pulls it down. The etymology of "surrender" means *to give up*, but we are not talking about surrender in the sense of quitting. When we surrender, we stop fighting, we stop fighting the natural flow of life and intended path, as the old proverb says, "If we are facing in the right direction, all we have to do is keep walking." Once we set upon an intended path, we can surrender and just enjoy the process as we move toward our intended goal. Although we often feel that we have to overwork the path and worry and over think and analyze the path, this only serves to impede us from the goal. We can give a hundred percent to something without fighting it or incessantly worrying about it, but we are in the habit of worry and fighting. Struggle has become a habit. So we bring it into our goals, often sabotaging our goals because it gets too heavy upon the path toward our intended goals. But the heaviness is just in the mind that worries, the mind that attempts to control. In reality, we can have an intended goal and do our best in each moment, but the fruits, the final result, is something we never really know even if we think we do. In fact, we do not even know if we will live out this hour, but we pretend that we know.

Control is a fear response: the fear that what we want may not show up drives us to micromanage our lives to the point of being control freaks. The paradox, though, is that the more we try to control, the less we feel in control: hence the worry and anxiety. We can ask ourselves, "What am I afraid of?" Because often the very thing we fear happening, we create to happen by meditating on it unconsciously all the time in the form of worry and anxiety. Remember our thoughts, our internal meditations, lead to action, and results follow. How, then do we let go and surrender? Well, the simple answer is that we just do, and the complicated answer is that it could be the toughest and simplest thing you ever do. But I guarantee it will be not only one of the most liberating things you do, but will help ensure your success in all you do. Once we set the intention or goal, we can practice being a hundred percent present and enjoy the process. In this way we will give a hundred percent to what we are doing. The irony of control is that it takes away from us doing our best, because we waste energy on the anxiety and worry and fear, making us less strong and less capable of giving a hundred percent. The ignorance of control is that we think without it we can't meet our goals, this is completely false. When we learn to surrender our fears of control, we then learn to be present and enjoy the bliss of the present moment. Control keeps us locked in future expectations. We can catch ourselves when we are doing this. When we find ourselves to be tense and worrisome, we can practice stopping. Maybe we can write it out until we have the realization that our controlling mind is actually impeding our success. All it takes is a change of perspective. We can cultivate patient acceptance as opposed to controlling fear. Learning to accept the moment for what it is gives us the power to surrender and create within that moment and work with the moment without needing to control it.

As the great Joseph Campbell once said,

> We're in a free fall into future. We don't know where we're going. Things are changing so fast, and always when you're going through a long tunnel, anxiety comes along. And all you have to do to transform your hell into a paradise is to turn your fall into a voluntary act. It's a very interesting shift of perspective and that's all it is... joyful participation in the sorrows and everything changes.

By bringing joy into the moment, we learn to participate in the game of life with joy. The more we do this, the more we will shift our habits from the control freak who enjoys little, to the skillful enjoyer who is confident in knowing his or her goals are obtainable and we need not attach and worry to make them happen.

Forgiveness and the Art of Letting Go

When we hear the word *forgiveness*, we associate it with letting some-one off the hook, a pardoning. Forgiveness, however, is a letting go, a surrender of painful emotions we tend to hold onto. We can begin the practice of forgiveness toward ourselves. We are so hard on ourselves, we self-hate, feel guilt and insecurity about things we have done or said or haven't done or said, whatever the situation may be. If we can learn to let go and forgive ourselves, be present and not hold onto the past or expectations of the future, then we will see the quality of our lives shift drastically. We can learn to say to ourselves, "I forgive you." We don't need to judge ourselves and cultivate guilt. We can let go of blame and learn to be kind to ourselves.

When we are harmed or offended by another, forgiveness is difficult to ex-tend. Forgiveness, however, does not mean we are letting the other person off the hook, it means that we let ourselves off the hook. We are not saying what they did or said to us was okay. Some people have had horrendous acts done to them by others: rape, robbery, murders of loved ones. When we learn to forgive another, we are not saying what they did was okay or letting them off the hook: we are letting ourselves off the hook. When we hold onto anger or sadness directed toward another, we are allowing them to still hurt us, even if we haven't seen them in decades or more. Holding onto anger only destroys us both physically and mentally. The Buddha explained that, "Holding onto anger is like drinking poison and expecting the other person to die." So in essence we are poisoning ourselves with the mind of anger and so forth. In fact, the brain lets out poison into the body in states of jealousy, anger, and so on. Forgiveness means we let go of the past and learn to live and enjoy the present more fully.

We often hold small grudges against people in our lives. The truth is we really never know someone else, we know only our idea of someone. Every time we see the person we are meeting someone new, yet our perceptions fix the person as being who we believe him or her to be. We are constantly changing, and although many people live up to the habits they have cre-ated, we only further foster those habits by relating to them as their habits. Learning to forgive ourselves and others is paramount in being able to live a joyful life in the present, not hung up on past pains or future fears.

CHAPTER 18
COMPASSION: THE UNIFYING FORCE

The Science of Compassion

The root of the word "compassion" can be broken up and described as followed. *Com* Latin for "with," and "passion" derived from the Latin *passus*, which is related to the English noun "patient," which means "one who suffers," so together it basically means *to suffer together*. Well this seems pretty grim but it's actually quite beautiful when we look at how this force alone can have immense unifying powers between all living beings. Three words I would like to open with are *compassion, kindness*, and *empathy*. Compassion is the deep wish for others not to suffer because we too have suffered or do suffer as they do, and kindness is the wish for them to be happy. Studies show that kind people are generally more successful at work, more popular, and have stronger immune systems. Basically, compassion is the understanding or empathy for another's suffering; it is the base of all love and a principal that can be found in all cultures, religious orders, philosophies, societies, and spiritual traditions and is present someplace within all living beings. Since every living being has or will suffer on some level in life, he or she can relate to the suffering of another. Empathy allows us to connect to another, destroying the separation between *you* and *me*, tearing down the walls of *self* and *other*. Our compassion unites us and allows us to deeply realize our interconnection with all. We become more generous as we see ourselves in another and will more readily help them, having felt this before. If compassion is based on empathy, and empathy requires we know our own hardship and suffering, then it is wise to start with ourselves. In fact the only way we can truly be compassionate to another is to learn compassion for ourselves.

Compassion for ourselves can begin by allowing our self to feel our suffering, to experience it instead of stuffing it down deep inside our subconscious and suppressing it and also without engaging in it and allowing it to destroy us. Instead of reacting to it, we can respond to it with compassion. In this way develop the habit for kindness toward ourselves: the wish for our self to be happy and free from suffering is far different than guilt, which is just feeling sorry for ourselves where we get caught in self-loathing and vilify our pains and suffering. This is not a kind act, for it only perpetuates the pain and suffering. If we view our painful emotions like a child, this may help. If we see a child in pain or suffering, we will not shut them away, and we shouldn't foster the pain by engaging in it and affirming it, which only further makes it worse. We wouldn't pick at a child's wound, but we pick at our own wounds. We agitate our own suffering. We can hold the child with care, and it's in this "care" where we begin to heal.

We are usually in the habit of doing the opposite, we shun the painful emotions and bury them or engage in them and allow them to fester and grow as we pick at them.

We can extend compassion and care toward our suffering without judgment or deeming them "bad," just being present and allowing ourselves to feel the pain in our body and mind. Then we can begin to bring wisdom (clear seeing) into it once it is calm. Like the child who screams and cries, we hold them with tenderness and when they settle we say, "See, it's not that bad, just a little cut." Now the child smiles and confidence ensues, but before, the drama of a deluded mind made a small cut on the knee into the most dramatic scene in human history. Often we endure more than a small cut on our knee. Often life gives us deep pains and deep wounds of mind and body, but we can always touch our suffering, hold it like the child, and practice compassion for our self. An analogy you hear often in Eastern philosophy is the one of a lotus growing out of mud. A lotus needs the mud in order to rise up and bloom into a beautiful flower. Likewise, our suffering begets our compassion and empathy, and now we can extend our beauty to the world in the form of understanding, our flower is our wisdom, our ability to see clearly when others cannot. And we see clearly because we have risen out of the same mud they are currently residing in.

Our suffering can awaken a deep well of compassion and love inside of us. Like the lotus in the mud, we can remind ourselves of this when we are suffering: we can say, "Out of this pain will arise compassion and understanding and kindness," and remember, people who are compassionate are generally stronger, not only in physical structure but in immune function as well. So the suffering will inevitably make us stronger.

Seeing the opportunity in it and realizing that we can transform all our pain into loving compassion for the benefit of not only ourselves but all beings gives us the strength to endure hard times.

Compassion helps us touch our fears, our anger, our jealousy and so forth. As we develop compassion for ourselves it becomes natural to feel it for others, even when we hadn't before. There is a natural well of compassion within us all, just waiting to be discovered. I believe that since we are all connected, we can tap into that compassion, even if we haven't been through exactly what another has been through. Any pain can create understanding because the basics are similar, we are suf- fering and want to be happy, so we can relate to that in others. When I was a child, and still to this day, I would never want to kill a bug or any living being for that matter. If there was a bug in the house and my mother told me to kill it, I would put it in a cup and put it outside. Whenever I would see others hurting animals or killing bugs, I would feel their pain. As I learned later, I am what they call an Empath, which means I can pick up on the feelings of others. Although my ability may have been more heightened than another who steps on a bug, not feeling it's pain, we all have these empathic abilities. We just have to learn to tap into them because we are all connected. Our ability to feel another's emotions is there, beyond the separation myth we build in our minds. I remember one time my cousin stepped on a frog, smashing it as it let out this final croaking squeak. I must have been about five years old. My heart sunk, and I felt such sorrow as I stood staring at the dead, smashed frog. My cousin ran off with no regard or care in the world. A great well of compassion welled up inside me, my wanting for another living being not to feel pain. And even though I wasn't a frog, and had never been stepped on, the compassion arose.

Our compassion can cripple us sometimes if we don't have the wisdom and clarity that goes along with it. In the beautiful tradition of Bud- dhism, they describe it like the two wings of a bird: one is the wing of compassion, and the other the wing of wisdom. We need both to fly, or else we just flop around in circles on the floor. When I first went to India and visited the state of Bihar, I was overwhelmed by the immense poverty and suffering there. Children who couldn't eat, people starving and missing limbs, dogs that were minutes from starvation fighting children for a bone in a garbage heap. I felt such deep compassion and also felt impotent to do anything. My compassion welled up so powerfully, that I felt I could do nothing to help this immense problem. I remember one day just sitting under a tree in the hot sun, feeling overwhelmed as tears streamed down my face. Now I had the compassion wing down, yet the wisdom was lacking. I realized later that although I could not help everyone here, I could help someone. The wisdom of Mother Teresa came to my mind, "I alone cannot change the world, but I can cast a stone across the waters to create many ripples." Upon my next trip to India I did much work on cultivating that wisdom wing and realized that as I worked on myself I was stronger and wiser to help others. I would see the overwhelming poverty and suffering all around me and would help whomever I could, sometimes just being an ear for another to vent to was enough.

We can all do "small things with great love," as Mother Teresa said. And if we all do small things every day, our collective effort to help others will add up to heal the entire world. We are all in this together, and our compassion is a unifying force that has the potential to heal everyone.

Compassion for Difficult People

We often feel uncomfortable being close to others, especially those we do not know. We are trained to be close to the select few we deem worthy of our closeness, and it's only because we do not know others, so there is a wall of fear there. After all it is others who we fight in wars, others who bring us pain in various ways. We create the good guy bad guy stories in every fabric of our culture, and so it is understandable why we are hesitant to be close to a stranger: after all we never know what the person may try to do to us. This way of looking at the world has created barriers of self and other, us and them. And although sometimes people do harm other people, the majority of us do not, and the majority of those who do, do so out of the deep pain of not being accepted and yearning the kindness and acceptance of others or out of delusion and ignorance such as greed and so forth.

Many times we encounter people who are seemingly difficult. Perhaps they express anger at us or say something rude to us or just do something that is annoying or frustrating to us that we dislike. Now our delusions of annoyance, frustration, anger, or whatever it may be arises, separating us from them. Remember, the delusions that the brain conjures up are primordially meant to protect the separate self. And so now we create the illusion of *enemy* on all its levels of an undesirable person to be around. When we realize that they are just suffering and seeking happiness like we are, we begin to let loose the strong grasp of delusion that starts wars, and we can allow compassion, not anger, to arise for another. In fact, compassion naturally arises when this wisdom is present. This does not mean we allow others to harm us with deed or word, but the harm is tenfold if we allow the festering of anger and hate on top of what was already done to mill in our minds. Compassion starts a healing process and gives us the courage to walk away with wisdom instead of reacting with anger, only serving to further the already painful situation. Can you see how the power of compassion can help us create in our lives? We can allow it to gives us the wisdom to step back and see the situation clearly, as opposed to allowing the delusion to make the reactive decision for us, resulting in usually more pain and delusion with both parties.

It isn't always easy feeling compassion for others. We often feel fear, resentment, disgust, hatred, and so on. In this situation we need to accept these feelings within us, those defensive feelings. Once we begin to do this, then compassion can begin to arise for the other. So again it must start with us. Often when another says or does something that irritates us, we allow the walls of reactions and defensive behavior to take over. We do this to ourselves as well, when a painful emotion or some conflicting emotion that frustrates us arises, we get defensive and annoyed at ourselves for feeling this way or acting in a certain way. We can practice stopping, letting go, and forgiveness, and in that space we create with letting go we are free to create whatever we wish to create.

A Simple Yet Powerful Compassion Meditation on Loving Kindness

We begin this meditation by just coming into a comfortable sitting position, positioning the hands however they feel comfortable, and gently closing the eyes. Scan the body from the top of the head to the palms of the feet and just recognize any areas of tension and allow them to melt away with your breath. Take a few deep breaths into the belly and just relax. Take a few moments to just relax and breathe, centering your mind and body. Once you have relaxed a bit, we can begin to contemplate. Bring your mind to someone you care about. Allow the feeling of the person's presence to be with you and feel the love you have for him or her. Perhaps this person is a small child, or a teacher who has inspired you, or anyone who ignites that feeling of love. Now reflect that everyone will suffer and feel pain in their lives, so allow the feeling of compassion to arise for this person. You can use a phrase such as "May you be free from pain and sorrow, may you be happy and joyful." Use their names if you wish, be intuitive and in the moment with your feelings of compassion. Hold this for a few minutes, this sincere wish for them to be happy and free from their pains and sorrows. Now shift the focus to yourself and offer the same phrases to yourself. "May I be free from pain and sorrow, may I be happy and joyful." Realizing that you too will feel pain and sorrow, you cultivate compassion for yourself and hold that for a few moments. Say these statements internally or softly out loud in any way that resonates with you, and once that feeling arises, just drop the analytical thinking and just hold that feeling of compassion for yourself. When the mind drifts off or if you lose that feeling again, use the saying or thinking and allow that feeling to arise again, searching and then finding that feeling and then simply drop the thoughts and hold the feeling of compassion for yourself as your point of meditation. After doing this for a bit, you can now shift your focus to someone you have had a difficult time with, someone who has frustrated you or brought that habit of anger out in you or whatever the situation might have been. Bring the person or situation to mind. Now reflect that this person too, just like you, wishes to be happy and free from sorrow and pain. And everything they do, including that which made you angry or frustrated, is also out of that wish to be happy and free from sorrow and pain in some form. So you can drop the anger or frustration and feel that connection with the person that he or she too, just like you, wishes to be happy. You can internally say, "May you (use his or her name if you like) be free from your sorrows and pain, may you be happy." Again allow that feeling of compassion to arise and then hold it as you have just done in the beginning here. Again hold this for a while, and when you lose it again, find it and hold it, just as we do in breath meditation, except the point of focus here is that feeling of compassion, wherever you feel it. After doing this for a bit, you can again shift your focus to a complete stranger. Perhaps someone at the checkout counter at the store, or someone from a newspaper article you just read, or a homeless person you may have seen. We do the same thing here: we realize that this person too, just like us, wishes to be happy and free from sorrows and pain. We can again say, "May you be happy and free from sorrow and pain." Again say or think this in any way that resonates with you and allows that feeling of compassion for a complete stranger to arise. Then just hold that feeling again as we have just done.

Within this meditation make it your own. Sometimes I picture a white light of joy coming from my heart and giving joy and happiness to the other person. Whatever it is that feels right for you, practice it. This simple meditation will have immense beneficial results for you if practiced with consistency. Remember to use the meditation techniques that best resonate with you. Use them all if you wish. Perhaps what you are feeling you need most that day, or perhaps you only use one. Be creative and remember to always have fun by bringing joy into the meditation.

CHAPTER 19
RIGHT ACTION, THE HEART OF MANIFESTING

The heart has its reasons of which reason knows nothing. ~ Blaise Pascal

We frequently hear people say, or read expressions such as, "follow your heart" or "live from the heart" and so forth, but what does this actually mean? We often associate the heart with matters of love and often with doing what is "right" for ourselves and others, a sort of universal love, if you will.

Many scientists, philosophers, and brilliant minds throughout history, including Aristotle, considered the heart to be the seat of reason and *true thought* and often rejected the value of the brain. The Stoics taught us that the heart is the seat of the soul. I have attended many lectures and retreats on the teachings of Buddha, and whenever they refer to the mind, they point to the chest in the area of the heart chakra. When I would sit in on lectures of Christianity the *sacred heart* is mentioned often, Jesus' physical heart is depicted as the representation of the divine love for all living beings.

The physical heart is indeed connected to our emotions, yet what I want to talk about is the deeper level of the heart, the energetic system that is connected to the highest vibration of perfection in this universe. This is the doorway into your higher self, or God, or Universe or whatever you would like to call it. This is where the physical human self can connect to the highest wisdom, and truth that is within you. Jesus taught us that, "the kingdom of God is within you." The Buddha taught us how to know "right action," how to live from the heart, and Carl Jung taught that, "your vision will become clear only when you look into your heart." We have all experienced this inner world of love, joy, and wisdom in our lives. Sometimes we tap into an intuitive truth. We just feel it is right, a profound sense of *knowing* and Oneness with all of the universe.

Often the heart does not seem logical at the moment of decision. It is not interested in win or lose, drama or fear, and many times it may seem to make irrational decisions. The heart resonates with the higher frequencies of perfection, omniscient if you will, whereas the brain often runs on lower frequencies of worry, doubt, and other dramatic fantasies. For this reason the brain is often at odds with the heart. We will know in an instant what is right action, but then the brain comes in and starts to question what the heart already knows to be the right answer, and because the heart does not engage in argument, the brain's yelling is what we hear, as opposed to the heart.

We have all experienced this before; we know to turn right, but we overthink it, then turn left, go way out of the way, then find our way back and realize that we knew to go right all along. This is a simplistic example. It is hard to pinpoint an example because all of our lives operate differently. In fact, perhaps the heart will bring us to the left turn, when the way to our destination is a right turn. The heart may know there is something down that left turn that we need to encounter before going onto the right turn. This sounds complicated, and it is if we overthink it. And that is what we are in the habit of doing: overanalyzing and thinking to death. This is the reason we need to learn to tap into the heart and allow it to guide us. Once we decipher the misguiding factors of delusional minds like fear and anger and greed, we can learn to know the language of the heart by easily seeing the frauds of delusion for what they are and smiling at them without engaging in them. When we talk about heart, we are not talking about the muscle, but the area of the heart, the energy center that resides in the chest but is not limited to the chest, the omniscient intuition we all have access to.

In any moment we can stop and ask, "What does my heart want?" In this way we begin to connect to the heart and develop a respect and relationship with our heart. And as we awaken the heart, it becomes easier to follow. The heart is like the perfect guidance system residing within us that will always lead us to *right action*. This is why the heart must be the captain and the brain the first mate. There is a place for the brain; it is a wonderful tool. Yet, it creates fantasy and drama in which the heart does not engage. As we begin to live our lives from the heart, we begin to develop a habit for doing so. When we live from the heart in our thinking and action, we will then be of the greatest benefit to not only ourselves but to all beings and the Earth. We can begin to develop the habit for listening and following our heart. At first it is not as easy to follow the heart, but the more we do it, the easier it becomes—like everything we do it becomes second nature. As we clear out our delusions and do the inner work, it will become easier to hear the heart and feel the heart's messages. We will begin to readily trust our heart's intuition or inner guide and surrender to it as we learn to trust.

It takes courage to live from the heart because it will often be against what the stirring of the brain would like to dictate, and many times will not conform to the ways of society, yet the more we do it the more our lives will become beneficial in every way. The more joy and abundance we will create and we will inevitably be living from the higher vibrations of truth for ourselves and all of the Earth.

How to Know Right Action and Live From the Heart

The more we are caught in the gross, superficial, world the less we delve into the heart. When our life is constantly motivated by our cravings and instant gratification, we begin to feel isolated and separate from what we truly need, always grasping insecurely at the surface. We must learn to be still and accept this moment and then dive deep into the heart and listen, for it speaks soft wisdom and will never lead you astray. When you learn to listen to your heart, you realize all of the answers you seek are there. In this way, you can tap into the psychic intuition of heart, and your confidence in direction will be strengthened. Here you will find an outline of meditation to foster your relationship with your heart. All of the meditations we have been practicing can be used whenever we feel necessary and be used together. For example we can do some basic breath meditation before engaging in this heart meditation or perhaps we use this as our daily meditation. Remember to make it your own. Delve into your practice in the way that resonates with your deepest truth and for the benefit of all, which includes you. We create a strong resolve to joyfully work on our self because life is a work in progress, and every moment is a beautiful creation.

A Meditation to Strengthen our Heart Connection

Come into your space of meditation. Scan the body and relax any tension and take a few deep breaths to settle the mind and body. Once you feel settled, move your focus from the head to the heart. You can visualize breathing light into the heart, igniting the heart. If you like, you can breathe in an emerald-green light, nourishing the heart center and the entire body with this emerald-green, healing radiance. Allow yourself to feel the vibration of the heart, and then just settle with that feeling. Try to quiet the brain. Feel the heartbeat, and every time your mind drifts to thoughts or noises, just bring your awareness back to the heart. Practice gently abiding with the heart and joyously nourishing your entire being with the healing vibration of the heart. Simply sit with the heart, opening to any sensations or messages it may have for you. If you like you can visualize pouring green or white light from the heart, connecting to hearts of all beings in the world and healing them with the limitless strength of your heart. Again make this meditation your own, and do what feels right. Allow the heart to lead the meditation. Simply sitting quietly and being with the heart will strengthen your connection with it, and in time you will more easily and effortlessly connect with it and be able to listen to and follow the heart. The heart whispers soft wisdom, so learn to be still and listen.

ABOUT
THE
AUTHOR

BRIAN E. MILLER

Brian E. Miller now has several books in print including *Shambhala* and *One More Chance*. Brian's teachings and writings entice us to delve deeply into the often dark recesses of the mind, discovering truths that can lead us to a more balanced, harmonious and purposeful life.

Realizing there are many paths and something to be learned from everyone and everything, Brian teaches from many sources. His passion to help others discover their limitless potential has led him to teach the science of meditation to anyone looking to overcome limiting beliefs and cultivate empowering habits in any arena of life. He has traveled all over the United States and India, amongst other parts of the world, studying and practicing intently with many renown and credible teachers and healers. He realizes that one's journey is that of self-exploration and expression and all he can do is be a medium for those wishing to search within for their own truth.

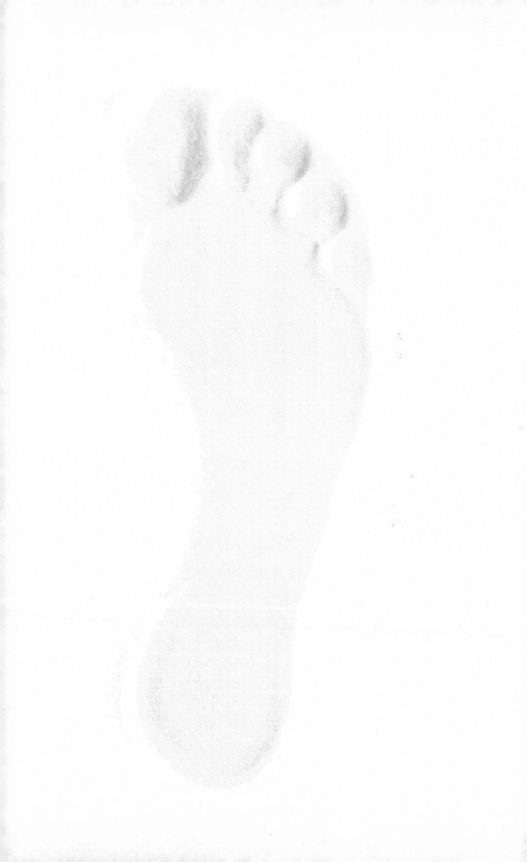